Tom Parker Bowles is an award-winning British food writer. He is the Restaurant Critic for *The Mail on Sunday* and writes a monthly column for *Country Life*. He is a regular judge on BBC's *Masterchef*, and is the author of eight books, including *Cooking and The Crown* and *Fortnum & Mason: The Cookbook*.

Let's Eat

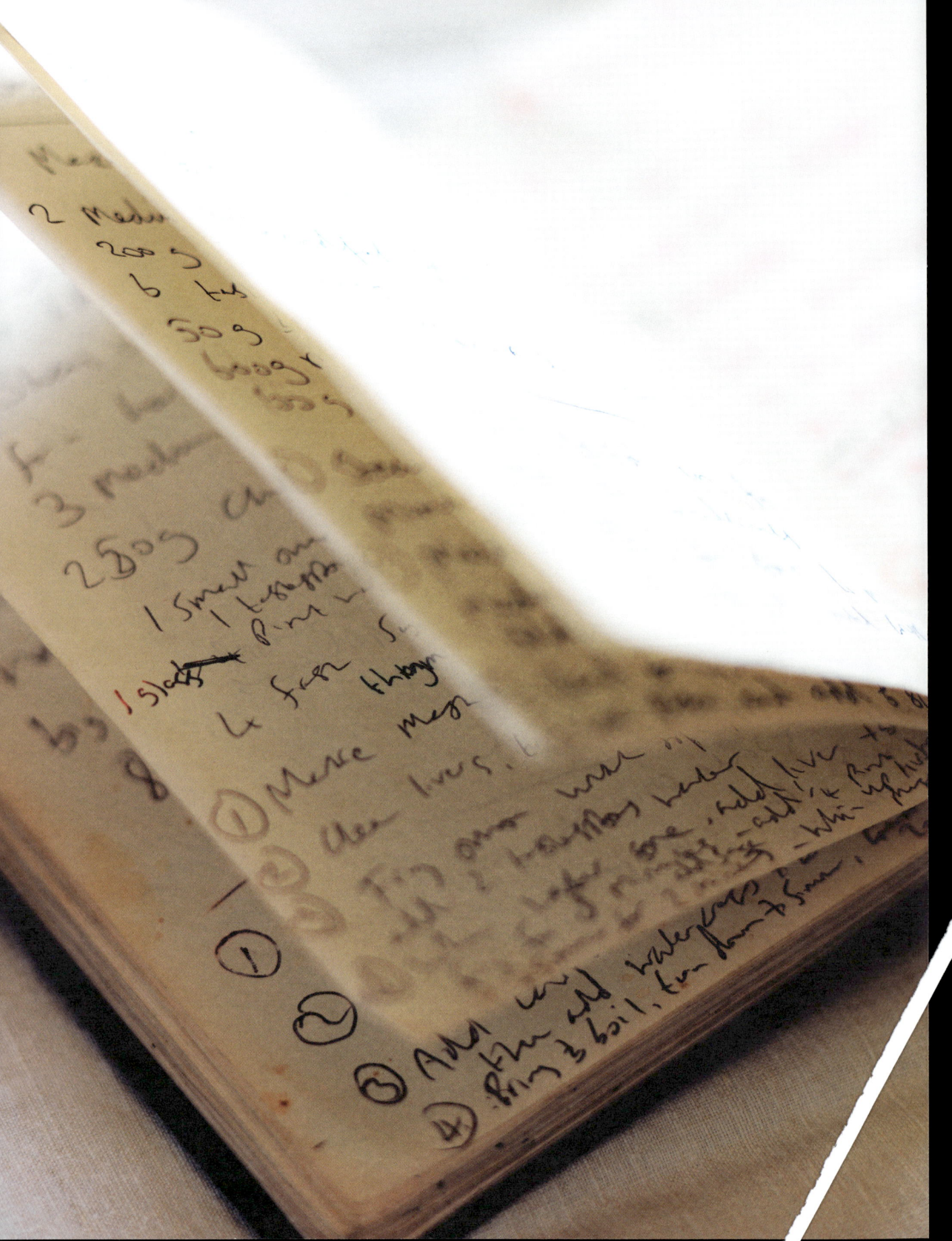

Let's Eat

Recipes from my kitchen notebook

Tom Parker Bowles

PAVILION

Acknowledgements

I'd like to thank the following, for their help, support, advice, recipes, photographs, design and inspiration: Cristian Barnett, Alex Bilmes, Luca del Bono, Caroline Buys, Antonio Carluccio, Richard Corrigan, Anne Dolamore, Ben Elliot, Alberto Figueroa, Matthew Fort, Gerard Greaves, Geordie Greig, Georgie Hewitt, Nigel Haworth, Fergus Henderson, Mark Hix, Simon Hopkinson, Reg Johnson, Sam Joiner, Bill Knott, Jeremy Lee, Sebastian Lee, Giorgio Locatelli, Laura Lopes, Justine Pattison, Polly Powell, Maggie Ramsay, Allan Sommerville, David Thompson, Ewan Venters and Fran Warde. As well as my mother and father; Grainne Fox, my ever-brilliant agent, and Becca Spry, who guided, edited and nurtured this book with a truly expert, elegant hand. And last of all to Sara, who continues to taste all the recipes with gilded palate and stoic expertise. As well as continuing to put up with me.

For Freddy

First published in the United Kingdom in 2012 by
Pavilion
An imprint of HarperCollins*Publishers* Ltd
1 London Bridge Street
London SE1 9GF

www.harpercollins.co.uk

HarperCollins*Publishers*
Macken House
39/40 Mayor Street Upper,
Dublin 1
D01 C9W8
Ireland

10 9 8 7 6 5 4 3 2 1

This edition first published in Great Britain by Pavilion
An imprint of HarperCollins*Publishers* 2025

Text © Tom Parker Bowles 2025
Design and layout © Pavilion 2025
Photography © Cristian Barnett 2025

Tom Parker Bowles asserts the moral right to be identified as the author of this work. A catalogue record of this book is available from the British Library.

ISBN 978-0-00-874370-3

For more information visit:
www.harpercollins.co.uk/green

Commissioning editor: Becca Spry
Design concept & cover: Georgina Hewitt
Photographer: Cristian Barnett
Home economist: Justine Pattison
Layout: Allan Sommerville
Copy editor: Maggie Ramsay
Stylist: Pene Parker
Production: Laura Brodie
Proofreader: Jamie Ambrose
Indexer: John Noble

Printed and bound by PaperCraft in Malaysia.

All rights reserved. No part of this publication may be reproduced, stored in a retrieval system or transmitted, in any form or by any means, electronic, mechanical, photocopying, recording or otherwise, without the prior written permission of the publishers.

This book is sold subject to the condition that it shall not, by way of trade or otherwise, be lent, re-sold, hired out or otherwise circulated without the publisher's prior consent in any form of binding or cover other than which it is published and without a similar condition including this condition being imposed on the subsequent purchaser.

This book contains FSC™ certified paper and other controlled sources to ensure responsible forest management.

{ Contents }

Introduction {6}

Comfort food {12}

Quick fixes {88}

Slow & low {148}

From far-flung shores {190}

Cooking for children {248}

Index {268}

Introduction

I have a battered old leather recipe book, dark blue and stained with fat, ketchup and chilli sauce. And this book provides most of the recipes for *Let's Eat*. Entry into this shabby journal is every bit as exacting as a stage with Thomas Keller or Marco Pierre White. Each recipe has to earn its place. The process goes as follows: I travel to Mexico City, Bangkok, Palermo, Bolton or Vientiane. And eat. Everywhere and everything, my belly swelling as the days go past.

I take copious, scrawled notes and jot down recipes on scraps of paper, everything from ticket stubs to napkins (and as anyone who has ever spent any time eating Asian street food knows, their napkins make loo roll seem like canvas). Once back at my desk in London I attempt to decipher the name of a dish hiding beneath an errant scrap of noodle. Or a local ingredient blurred by a dousing of beer.

Yet this is not simply a traveller's tome, but a collection of very British recipes, too. The food I grew up eating, and still adore. The shepherd's pies and grilled sole, fresh asparagus and roasted grouse that never cease to thrill and delight.

At home, I cook each recipe at least three times, endlessly amending until it works (and gets the seal of approval from my wife; seriously, when she nods, the whole world agrees). Then, and only then, is it transcribed into the book. As the years pass, comments and additions find their way onto the pages. I love this leather volume, as much as I love my much-abused wok. Both have the patina of time and constant use, dirty and ragged to the outsider, but utterly beautiful to me. This book, like the wok, tells the story of my love of food. The scribbled additions, the infantile representations of the perfect-sized meatball and the scrawled notes, illegible to anyone but myself.

Let's Eat doesn't set out to sharpen your knife skills, nor redefine the way you view food. Taste takes precedence over pretty presentation and I've little time for pious finger-wagging. Buy the best you can afford. Good free-range meat does cost more. The animals take longer to grow, are killed later, and are hung (in the case of beef) often for longer than a month. This means extra cash, sure. As well as extra flavour. And an immeasurably happier life for those beasts, too. But having promised I wouldn't, I'm starting to lecture from the lofty heights of my food writer's ivory tower.

The same goes for those endlessly repeated mantras of seasonal and local. Of course seasonal food is important, as this quarterly demarcation brings changes to the market and kitchen that never cease to delight. I passionately believe that the first British asparagus, arriving in late spring, is worth hanging on for, the taste made all the better by the nine-month wait, served with good melted butter and a sprinkling of salt. The same goes for grouse in August, native oysters in September (one drop of Tabasco, one of lemon), gull's eggs in May and strawberries in June. As one ingredient shuffles off for another year, it's replaced by something equally beguiling. But I can't bear those boorish types who scream bloody murder if you eat an apple in spring.

I'm all for local food, too, but don't start quivering with rage at the thought of air-freighted fruits and fancies. Our diet would be pretty dull without the likes of lemons and pepper, chocolate and coffee, rice and fish sauce. And is it really so evil to prefer a glossy, firm onion grown 100 miles away to some rotten, squidgy specimen from that crap shop down the road? Pragmatism is the key, not po-faced gloom.

Too often, cookbooks are written by chefs who've long forgotten the constraints of the home kitchen. I promise that there'll be no recipe starting with the instruction, 'Take 30 litres of veal stock …' or 'Dip the whole pine nuts into the pine nut praline and then dip them into the liquid nitrogen …' Most of us hardly have room for a mini-blender, let alone a Pacojet processor or *sous-vide* bath.

Over the years, I've cooked every recipe in this book in my own kitchens. Some of them were no bigger than the average store-cupboard. If you can soften onions on the wonky electric ring of a canary yellow Baby Belling with only two settings – searing and Hades – then you can do anything.

For me, cooking is so much more than the application of heat to ingredients. It makes me happy; from the planning and shopping to the preparation and eating. With the radio trilling away in the background and a glass of wine at my right hand, I feel as if all is well in the world: cooking as catharsis, as ritual, as bliss. Plus there's the ironically selfish pleasure that cooking for others can bring: friends and family all gathered around the table. 'Why is it that young couples buy a television or sofa before a table?' is a question that vexes chef Fergus Henderson. And quite rightly so.

Food is not just mere 'lifestyle'. It's our one shared universal experience. You can be celibate, teetotal and tax-dodging, but you still have to eat. It's the basis of all economies, the catalyst for wars and the keeper of peace. The move from hunter-gatherer to sedentary farmer saw the birth of civilisation as we know it. And the history of a country, of its invasions and conquests, is far better illustrated through the food we eat than through some dusty, desiccated historical tome.

Food, too, is the great communicator. My grasp of foreign tongues is shaky, to say the least. Yet the symbol of enjoyment, the rubbing of one's gut, is universal. One gets to see far more of an alien culture from behind a robata grill, zinc bar or home-made smoker than from any number of insipid guidebooks.

All the dishes in this book are within easy reach of anyone who can turn on an oven and grasp a knife. I'm a resolutely amateur cook, my culinary education untainted by years spent in restaurant kitchens. I'm messy and bumbling, with presentation generally more suited to Bedlam than Bocuse. These, though, are recipes to make the taste buds grin and the belly cheer.

Let's Eat takes the choicest cuts from ten years spent as a professional food writer, and throws it into one volume. I've banged on enough. Let's eat.

{ Comfort food }

'Landlord, bring us beans and bacon,
and a bottle of your finest Burgundy.'

G K Chesterton

If beans, bacon and Burgundy don't ooze comfort, then God only knows what does. Comfort food is familiar, without fuss, drama or pomp. Straightforward, reliable and ever welcome, this is the Ronseal of recipe types: 'Does exactly what it says on the tin.' It's all about easy pleasure and solid flavours, an edible balm that tastes exactly as it should.

It is, though, the most subjective of culinary categories, as the choice of dish is defined entirely by one's gastronomic past. A childhood spent tugging the apron strings of a great English cook will produce markedly different dishes to a youth passed alongside wok and cleaver. Yet anyone with a heartbeat and opposable thumb will have at least one dish – be it hot buttered toast, red lentil dhal or peppered tripe soup – that coddles, comforts and soothes.

The majority of dishes here are European in genesis, as comfort food is particularly well suited to temperate climes; a later chapter deals with food from far-off lands too. There's a good sprinkling of British food. These are the staple dishes of my youth, adolescence and adult life. A week will rarely pass when I don't cook at least one of these recipes. Bonhomie for the belly and succour for the soul.

{ Cooking at home }

'Heat is just another form of seasoning,' I was once told by that Celtic force of nature, chef Richard Corrigan. This is a man whose intelligence is matched only by his generosity and, as ever, he's spot on. The flavour and texture of a piece of meat is affected by the amount of heat used, from quick sear to slow simmer. Yet too often the amateur cook fears real heat. We soften our onions on a piddling flame, and complain that it takes 30 minutes, not ten. We're afraid of burning our meat, rather than browning it. And we struggle with gas that seems to have only two settings: nothing and too hot.

Experience is everything, and the more that I cook and learn, the easier things become. I still panic at the thought of hollandaise sauce, for example, yet soufflés hold no fear. It doesn't help when chefs tell us how easy everything is, forgetting that they can bone chickens in their sleep, whereas I'd rather braise my own nose than attempt it again.

Professional chefs do have many advantages: when they dry-fry chillies, they have extractor fans that are so powerful they rip the words straight from their lips. No question of gassing out the house as it does at home. Nor do they have to contend with the smell of burnt dripping hanging around the sitting room for weeks after cooking huge portions of boeuf Bourguignon. Or the stench of chip fat clinging tenaciously to every fibre. They can blacken steaks to their hearts' content, flambé duck without fear of ruining the ceiling and fling the fat with reckless abandon. That is the point of a professional kitchen.

At home, things must be a little more subdued, but it's never quite as calm as the blessed Delia might suggest. She makes it look easy, as she's been doing what she does, beautifully, for many years. All I'm saying is that cooking is often messy, smelly, noisy and painful. That a pan full of hot fat will always spit like a cobra when introduced to a handful of raw meat. And sharp knives continue to slice open even the most lauded of hands. Don't fear the heat, and cooking suddenly becomes a whole lot more easy.

{ Fat }

Once upon a time, in the not-so-distant past, we worshipped fat. Fat was health, wealth and happiness. 'The fat of the land' was something to be coveted rather than disdained. We hankered after great wobbling dollops of marrow, gleaned from the bone with a specially shaped scoop. Fought over the last scrap of chicken skin. And lusted after lard, dripping, suet, schmaltz and butter. Fat carries flavour and aroma, provides the sexiest of textures, allows us to relish in our meat and delight in our food. Without fat, life would be one long lunch with Hare Krishnas.

Fat is also utterly essential to human life: our brains wouldn't function without the stuff, our cells would cease to survive, join the bleedin' choir invisible. Hormones would wither and die, immune systems buckle.

If the body were allowed to choose its fuel, it would go for fat, no question. Fat provides double the energy of similar amounts of protein and carbohydrates. Yet 50 years back, saturated fat suffered a spectacular fall from grace: from hero to zero in a matter of months. Scientists noted that coronary heart disease had suddenly become the biggest killer of all. At the same time, after the bleak paucity of the rationing years, there was an increased consumption of animal fats. No surprises there. Fourteen years of mock goose and Woolton pie will do that to an appetite. Scientists put two and two together and came up with four and a half. More animal fats, more heart disease, ergo animal fat is a gimlet-eyed, stone-cold killer. Animal fats became Public Enemy Number One. Despite the fact that there has been no conclusive proof linking saturated fat with heart disease, fat's image was changed for ever.

That's not to say that one could survive solely on a diet of butter, bone marrow, lard and milkshakes. Too much of anything, from rice cakes to lardy cakes, is never a good thing. The palate would start to tire and the body bloat. A healthy diet means a balanced diet, lots of green stuff, nuts, pulses, fish and the rest. Fat doesn't kill; rather, too much of the wrong kind can. Allied with sitting on your vast, wobbling butt all day, munching Quavers by the ton and slurping entire reservoirs of Cherry 7-Up. So in short, embrace animal fats, revel in them, but don't exist solely upon them. And buy the very best you can afford. Fat you can see, wrapped around kidneys or hugging a leg of lamb, is not the stuff to worry about. It's those hidden buggers, creeping around all those processed foods, that are the truly dangerous foe.

'Fat carries flavour and aroma, provides the sexiest of textures, allows us to actually relish in our meat and delight in our food.'

Spaghetti with meatballs

{ SERVES 4 }

500 g/1 lb 2 oz minced pork
250 g/9 oz minced steak or beef
1 whole egg and 1 yolk
85 g/3 oz breadcrumbs, soaked in 125 ml/4 fl oz milk for 10 minutes, then squeezed out
2–5 dried chillies, crumbled
sea salt and freshly ground black pepper
2 tablespoons olive oil
500 g/1 lb 2 oz dried spaghetti
grated Parmesan, to serve

For the sauce
2 tablespoons olive oil
1½ onions, finely chopped
1-3 fresh Thai or finger chillies, finely chopped
1 clove garlic, finely chopped
2½ x 400 g/14 oz cans chopped tomatoes
8 basil leaves, torn

Italian-American food at its best, star of more mob movies than you can shake a *cannoli* at. Purists may argue that *Goodfellas*, Martin Scorsese's red-sauce-splashed classic, was the meatball's greatest ever cinematic moment. 'Veal, beef, pork …' mumbles Vinnie, cooking up his prison feast. 'You gotta have the pork. That's the flavour.' As well as cutting the garlic with a razor blade. But it's actually in *Point Break*, Kathryn Bigelow's brilliant surf, screw, run and rob film, where the meatball reaches its peak. So fine is the sandwich that it actually causes the cops, who are on stakeout, to miss the bank being robbed. When done well, meatballs have that sort of effect.

To make the meatballs, mix the pork, beef, egg, egg yolk, breadcrumbs and chillies together with a good pinch of salt and lots of pepper, then cover and chill for 30 minutes (the mixture, not you).

Meanwhile, to make the sauce, heat the oil in a saucepan, add the onions, chillies and garlic and cook gently until soft. Add the tomatoes, season, and simmer uncovered for 40 minutes. Add the basil at the end of cooking time.

Roll the meat mixture into small, squash-ball-sized balls. Heat the olive oil over a medium-high heat in a frying pan and fry the meatballs for 2–3 minutes, leaving the inside a little underdone.

Cook the spaghetti in a large saucepan of boiling lightly salted water, following the timing on the pack. Five minutes before the spaghetti is ready, add the meatballs to the sauce and simmer for 5 minutes, until cooked. Drain the pasta and serve with the meatballs, sprinkled with Parmesan.

Chilli cottage pie

{ SERVES 6 }

2 tablespoons olive oil
½–2 Scotch bonnet chillies, finely chopped
4 red onions, finely chopped
1 kg/2 lb 2 oz minced beef (freshly minced if possible)
2 tablespoons tomato purée
4 teaspoons Worcestershire sauce, or to taste
Tabasco
500 ml/18 fl oz fresh beef stock (you can use cubes at a push)
sea salt and freshly ground black pepper

For the mash
8 large Maris Piper potatoes, about 1.3 kg/3 lb total weight, scrubbed
6 tablespoons milk
50 g/1¾ oz butter, plus 25 g/1 oz to dot on top

Too often, the cottage pie (and its bleating cousin, the shepherd's pie) is a mean sort of lunch, made with small, rubbery pellets of cheap mince, a splash of ketchup and lumpy mashed potato. Even worse, people insist on using the leftovers from Sunday's roast. I'm all for using up chicken bones and the like, but to chop up yesterday's beef for a pie not only gives an inferior filling – it robs me of roast beef sandwiches too. My great-grandfather, food writer and polemicist P Morton Shand, blamed the decline of British food on our culture of leftovers, where '… the joint lingered from Sabbath to Sabbath, suffering diverse strange transformations in its progress from Sunday's midday dinner to Saturday's supper: hot, cold; cold, hashed; cold, minced; cold, rissoles; cold, shepherd's pie; cold, Kromensky; and cold, stewed. It is the very diagnosis of dyspepsia.' I agree. This recipe uses fresh beef mince. If you can get the decent stuff from your butcher, freshly minced, it does make all the difference. This is a cheap dish, but shouldn't be a mean one. Avoid 'lean' mince at all costs.

As to chillies, I like a good kick of warmth, not so much that it sends diners fleeing from the table, their tongues sizzling in bowls of yogurt. I use one or two Scotch bonnets, but adapt as needed. They're pretty fiery, but have a lusciously fruity tang. If you do have to use those generic Dutch big chillies, good luck. They have all the kick of a limbless ass.

For the mash, I don't bother peeling the potatoes before cooking. Boil in their skins, leave to cool, then peel by hand. Much quicker and easier.

Gently heat the oil in a heavy-bottomed saucepan and soften the chillies in it (do open a window, as these chillies can create a gas that tends to get children crying and wives hacked off), then add the onions and soften for about 10 minutes.

Add the beef, turn the heat to high and brown it. Add the tomato purée and cook for 2 minutes. Add the Worcestershire sauce, a few jigs of Tabasco and the stock; taste, then season. Bring to the boil, reduce the heat to low and simmer for 25 minutes. Preheat the oven to 180°C/350°F/Gas 4.

Meanwhile, make the mash. Put the potatoes in a big pan of lightly salted water, bring to the boil, then simmer for 20–25 minutes, until a knife goes through with ease. Tip into a colander, let them cool a little, then peel. Heat the milk and butter in a small saucepan until the butter melts, then mash the potatoes with the mixture. Season.

Take a rectangular pie dish and pile in the hot meat. Top with mash. Fork the top of the mash so it looks like a choppy sea. Dot with a little extra butter and bake for 20–30 minutes, until the top is golden and the meat bubbling fiercely below. Serve with boiled peas.

Beef Stroganoff

{ SERVES 4 }

600 g/1 lb 5 oz fillet steak, cut into 5-cm/2-inch-long strips
sea salt and freshly ground black pepper
1 teaspoon hot paprika
about 75 g/3 oz butter
1 tablespoon plain flour
100 ml/3½ fl oz chicken stock
1 tablespoon tomato purée
1 teaspoon French mustard
115 g/4 oz small mushrooms, sliced
1 onion, finely chopped
75 ml/2½ fl oz dry white wine
200 ml/7 fl oz soured cream
2 tablespoons finely chopped flat-leaf parsley
boiled long-grain rice and green salad, to serve

There are endless arguments as to the origins of beef Stroganoff – whether it was a Hungarian dish, a classic Russian one, or a French one, inspired by Russia. The Stroganovs were a rich and wealthy family of merchants, traders with a long geographical reach. And one of the clan was said to have employed a French chef who is reputed to have created the dish. Other experts disagree, citing the etymology as derived from *strogat*, meaning in Russian to 'cut into pieces.' The truth is long lost. What remains, though, is a dish that uses soured cream and paprika. Well, sometimes. In other recipes, it uses cream instead. Some marinate the meat, others don't. There is no real 'authentic recipe' and this one most certainly isn't. But it's broadly recognisable and tastes damned good too.

Toss the strips of steak in salt, pepper and paprika, cover and put in the fridge for 2 hours.

Melt 25 g/1 oz of the butter in a small saucepan over a medium heat, stir in the flour and cook for 2–3 minutes to make a golden brown roux. Gradually blend in the stock, tomato purée and mustard, bring to the boil, then simmer for 5–10 minutes until thickened. Set aside.

Heat another 25 g/1 oz butter in a large frying pan over a medium-high heat and cook the mushrooms for a few minutes. Scoop them out of the pan onto a plate and set aside. Cook the onion in the same pan, adding more butter if needed, then add to the plate of mushrooms. Cook the steak in the remaining butter until browned on all sides, about 3–4 minutes. Deglaze the pan with the wine.

Return the mushrooms and onions to the pan, along with the sauce and soured cream. Mix well, then cover and let stand for 15 minutes. Reheat, sprinkle with chopped parsley, and serve with rice and a green salad.

The perfect burger

There's a lot of guff talked about hamburgers: adding eggs or onions to the mix and topping them with pineapple, beetroot, foie gras and God knows what else. I've travelled across America in search of burger perfection and found that one rule applies – the simpler the burger, the better. You still need good meat, minced rump or sirloin with about 20 per cent fat, preferably from a butcher. And a small, soft bun that can be held in one hand. Lettuce, tomato, cheese and bacon are all acceptable, even desirable, additions, not forgetting proper pickles, too. One of the best I've ever eaten was at the In-N-Out burger chain in California. Simple, succulent and perfect. Byron's Britain's best chain. For now, anyway. But don't mess about. No monster-size patties or wacky embellishments; just something to be wolfed in about four or five bites, the juices dribbling down your chin.

{ MAKES 8 }

sea salt and freshly ground black pepper
1 kg/2 lb 2 oz minced beef, with at least 20% fat
8 slices Cheddar or Swiss cheese
16 rashers smoked streaky bacon
8 soft white buns, split
2 beef tomatoes, sliced
1 iceberg lettuce
4 large sweet pickles, halved
mayonnaise, ketchup and mustard, to serve

Add a good pinch of salt to the beef, and lots of pepper, mix, cover and leave in the fridge for an hour.

Shape the mixture into 8 patties. Heat a heavy-based pan or barbecue to high, then cook the burgers for about 3 minutes on each side for rare, 4 minutes for medium and 6 for well done. A minute before they're ready, top them with cheese so it melts slightly.

Fry the bacon until crisp and toast the buns on the cut sides for 30 seconds.

Now the build. Bottom bun, then burger and cheese, then 2 rashers of bacon, a slice of tomato, a couple of lettuce leaves and a pickle half. Leave it to personal taste when it comes to the mayo, ketchup and mustard. Then top bun.

Toad in the hole

{ SERVES 4 }

115 g/4 oz plain flour
2 medium eggs, beaten
sea salt and freshly ground black pepper
300 ml/½ pint full-fat milk
3 tablespoons lard or olive oil
450 g/1 lb good pork sausages

One of the very few school dishes, along with the ersatz ribs and crisps on a Sunday, that I actually found edible. A thrifty lunch, sure, but make sure you get the best sausages you can find (I like chipolatas for this) and it becomes a very decent feast. This is my late step-mother Rose's recipe. She specifies lard, quite rightly, as it adds to the flavour. But olive oil will do fine.

Preheat the oven to 220°C/425°F/Gas 7. Sift the flour into a bowl, mix in the eggs and season. Whisk in the milk to make a smooth batter.

Put 2 tablespoons lard or olive oil into a frying pan over a medium heat, then cook the sausages until you have a good colour.

Put the remaining lard or olive oil into a 18 x 28 cm/ 7 x 11 inch baking tray or roasting tin and put into the oven for a few minutes, until smoking. Pour one-third of the batter into the tray. When it starts to rise and set in the hot oil, arrange the sausages in it and pour over the rest of batter. Bake for 25–30 minutes, until the batter is browned and billowing.

Roast woodcock

Beguiling brown eyes, an elegant, rapier-like beak and delicate black markings – the woodcock is an undoubtedly beautiful bird. Agile as a housefly and very hard to shoot. The eating is rather less refined. It arrives at the table roasted whole, neck lolling and eye staring blindly up. The skull is hewn in half to get at the brains, while the innards lie thick on a piece of fried bread. The flesh is rich, dark, with a hint of the pungent. For those who adore their game, it's the best of the lot.

Any shot bird will have a clean gut (they empty their bowels as they fly), and the entrails are soft and livery in taste. I buy my birds from The Blackface Meat Company (www.blackface.co.uk). This is based on a recipe from Hugh Fearnley-Whittingstall's magisterial *The River Cottage Meat Book* (Hodder & Stoughton 2004).

{ SERVES 1 }

1 woodcock, plucked but not drawn, head on
a little soft butter
sea salt and freshly ground black pepper
2 rashers streaky bacon
a little red wine
1 slice of good crusty white bread, halved

Remove the gizzard: either ask your butcher to do this, or make a small split in the vent end of the bird, insert a finger and feel for a hard little lump. Spear it with a cocktail stick, pull it out, snip it off and push the intestines back into the body.

Preheat the oven to 230°C/450°F/Gas 8. Put the bird in a roasting tin, massage butter over the breast and season. Lay the bacon over the breast, then tuck the head and neck under the wing and put in the hot oven for 8–20 minutes: 8 gives you bloody, 20 well done (I like about 10 minutes). Remove the bacon after 5 minutes, chop and set aside.

Rest the bird on a warmed plate for 10 minutes. Using a teaspoon, carefully scoop out the innards and set aside. In a small frying pan, heat a little butter and add the bacon. Sizzle for a minute or two, then add the innards and juices from the roasting tin. Add a little red wine, bubble gently for 2 minutes, season and mash any lumpy bits. Toast the bread, then spread the 'pâté' on one half and rest the bird on the other. Gnaw off every last scrap of meat.

Roast grouse

{ SERVES 4 }

4 young grouse (I get mine from www.blackface.co.uk)
50 g/1¾ oz butter, softened
sea salt and freshly ground black pepper
150 ml/5 fl oz dry white wine
300 ml/10 fl oz game or chicken stock
sprig of thyme
watercress, to serve

For the fried breadcrumbs
200 g/7 oz white bread, a couple of days old, crusts removed
50 g/1¾ oz butter

A truly seasonal British treat. I start to get the urge round about the end of July, and by 12th August, when the season starts, I'm craving my first taste. When you have a young bird, it would be heresy to do anything other than roast it, with all the traditional trimmings: clear gravy, fried breadcrumbs and bread sauce. There's no need for bacon, as it tends to overwhelm the delicate taste.

As to hanging, I don't believe the young birds need it. The Victorians had a taste for birds so 'high' that the maggots were already feasting, and the flesh was horribly bitter. Forget all that. The young grouse is a spectacularly unthreatening beast: sweet, succulent and wonderful. I like mine pink, but not gushing blood. And my father reckons that cold grouse makes the greatest breakfast of all.

Preheat the oven to 240°C/475°F/Gas 9. Lightly cover the grouse breasts with butter and season inside and out. Put into the searing hot oven for about 15 minutes. You want rare meat, not bloody. The breasts should feel fairly firm. If too soft, they're not cooked. Remove the bird from the tin, and leave to rest while you make the gravy.

Meanwhile, to make the breadcrumbs, tear the bread into small bits and blitz in a food processor to make crumbs. Fry the breadcrumbs in the butter over a medium heat until crisp. Drain on kitchen paper, then season.

Pour off the excess fat from the roasting tin, then put the tin over a high heat and throw in the wine, stirring and scraping while you simmer it. Reduce by half, then add the stock, thyme, salt and pepper and boil to reduce until deeply flavoured. Add any of the juices released from the resting grouse, then strain through a sieve into a warm jug. Serve with watercress, fried breadcrumbs and bread sauce (see page 28).

Bread sauce

{ **MAKES 600 ML/20 FL OZ** }

1 onion, halved
6 cloves
500 ml/18 fl oz milk
2 bay leaves
sea salt and freshly ground
  black pepper
200 g/7 oz white bread, a couple
  of days old, crusts removed
100 ml/3½ fl oz double cream

Steaming, and stained dark brown with gravy, bread sauce adds beauty and ballast to whatever it touches. Which is usually chicken or turkey, as any other meats tend to overpower its subtle, clove-scented allure. The key lies in infusing the milk with onion and spices.

Stud the onion with the cloves and put it into a saucepan with the milk, bay leaves, salt and pepper. Bring to the boil, then take off the heat and leave to stand for 30 minutes.

Tear the bread into small bits and blitz in a food processor to make rough crumbs. Remove the onion and bay leaves from the milk, add the breadcrumbs and bring gently back to the boil, then simmer over a low heat for about 20 minutes, giving it the occasional stir.

Pour in the cream, bring back to a simmer and whisk, then serve immediately.

Pot roast chicken

This dish is near impossible to bugger up. The initial browning (to add that extra level of flavour) tends to spit viciously and takes longer than you think. One breast, then the other, then onto its back. Stock cubes are fine, as there's so much else going on, but if you do use them cut back on the salt.

This is something that's developed over the years. I added the soy and rice wine because they were there and it seemed a good idea at the time. And it worked. The wine gives a rounded, rich sweetness while the soy deepens the flavour of the broth. Don't fear the excess amount of garlic. The cloves soften and mellow in the juices.

{ SERVES 2–4 }

2 tablespoons olive oil
1 x 1.5 kg/3–4 lb chicken
   (the best you can afford)
1 lemon, halved
150 ml/5 fl oz dry white wine
10 cloves garlic, unpeeled
2 big sprigs of rosemary
350 ml/12 fl oz chicken stock
   (fresh or cube)
4 tablespoons Shaoxing
   rice wine
2 tablespoons soy sauce
handful of coriander stalks
2 pinches of cayenne pepper
   (optional, but gives it a
   wonderful heat)
sea salt and freshly ground
   black pepper
thick slices of brown bread,
   to serve
cos lettuce salad, to serve

Preheat the oven to 180°C/350°F/Gas 4. Heat the olive oil in a large cast-iron pan over a medium-high heat and brown the chicken all over, about 10 minutes. Remove the chicken. Shove half the lemon up its ass and squeeze the other half over the skin. Deglaze the pan with the white wine, stirring, then put the chicken back in. Add the garlic, rosemary, stock, rice wine, soy sauce, coriander stalks, cayenne, salt and pepper. Bring to the boil.

Cover and roast for 1 hour 10 minutes to 1 hour 20 minutes. To test the chicken is cooked, poke a skewer into the thickest part of the thigh: the juices should be golden, not pink.

Transfer the chicken to a plate and leave to rest for 10 minutes. In the meantime, strain the cooking liquid through a sieve into another pan; discard the herb stems, but squeeze all the garlic through. Remove excess fat from the top with a spoon, then boil until the liquid is reduced by a third.

Carve the chicken and place in bowls atop a slice of bread. Pour over your sauce and eat with a crisp, simple cos lettuce salad. Drink any excess sauce direct from your bowl.

Comfort food

A deeply healthy, utterly addictive noodle dish

{ SERVES 2 }

2 chicken breasts (the best you can afford), cut into 1 cm/ ½-inch cubes

juice of 1 lime

2 teaspoons *gochujang* (Korean chilli paste) or a good whack of fish sauce, 2 tiny chopped bird's eye chillies and a splash of soy sauce

For the stir-fry

250 g/9 oz Thai rice noodles

dash of groundnut oil

3 cloves garlic, finely chopped

4 spring onions, sliced into 2.5 cm/1 inch pieces diagonally

½ head of broccoli (about 140 g/ 5 oz), cut into small florets

8 Thai or banana shallots, finely sliced

8 baby corn, quartered

50 g/1¾ oz frozen peas

50–100 ml/2–4 fl oz chicken stock (a cube is fine)

3–10 bird's eye chillies, finely chopped (depending how hot you like it)

2 teaspoons fish sauce

big handful of coriander leaves, roughly chopped

small handful of mint leaves, roughly chopped

1 lime, halved

This is probably the dish I cook more than any other, and we eat it at least twice a week at home. There was much debate as to whether it belonged in the From far-flung shores chapter, but in the end I decided this was comfort, pure and simple. Eating it makes me happy, wholesome even.

You can use whatever vegetables you have to hand, from frozen peas to broccoli, sugar snaps, French beans or bean sprouts. It even makes that ridiculous baby corn look useful. The key is a balance between the hot, sour and salty. The flavours are bold, but never overwhelming.

It's the sort of food that renders talking irrelevant. Just writing about these noodles makes my mouth water. My wife describes them as 'medicinal', thanks to all the fresh vegetables, herbs and chillies within. We like it hot, but tone down the chillies if need be. And you can always add more heat, by way of the chillies in the fish sauce. If you can't get hold of those fiendish little scud or bird's eye chillies, use a quarter of the amount of habanero or Scotch bonnet. The flavour is different, but the heat mighty.

There are two slightly exotic ingredients here, both easily available on the internet (www.royalthaisupermarket.com) or from Asian shops. They make the dish better still, but are not essential. The first is *gochujang*, a Korean fermented chilli paste that I use in the marinade. It has a deep, rich flavour with a hint of Marmite. And the second are the noodles I use (Khanom Jeen Rice Noodles 200g), specialist noodles used by the Thais for breakfast and curries. They have a wonderful soft texture. If you can't get them, use any rice noodles. I have a pair of special white bowls we use for this soup, deep and wide. They are as much a part of the ritual as are the noodles themselves.

{ CONTINUES OVERLEAF }

For the chilli fish sauce

75 ml/2½ fl oz fish sauce

4–8 bird's-eye chillies, finely chopped

juice of 1 lime

This is best cooked in a wok, and the chicken must be cut into small cubes of roughly the same size, to ensure they cook evenly. Make it in two batches. The actual cooking takes a few minutes. Once the prep is done, you're laughing.

Put the chicken in a bowl with the lime juice and *gochujang*. Cover and leave to marinate in the fridge for an hour. Remove from the fridge 10 minutes before cooking.

To make the chilli fish sauce, mix all the ingredients together and set aside.

For the stir-fry, cook the rice noodles in a large pan of boiling water according to the packet instructions. Drain, cool under cold running water and set aside.

Drain the chicken, discard the marinade, and pat the chicken dry with kitchen paper.

Heat the groundnut oil in a wok until smoking, then throw in half the garlic, cook for a second, then add half the chicken and stir until browned, about 1–2 minutes.

Add half of all the vegetables, but not the chillies. Stir-fry for another 30 seconds, then add half the stock and chillies. Taste, season with fish sauce and cook for a further 30 seconds to a minute, until the chicken is cooked through. Add half the herbs, mix and add half the noodles. Mix for another 30 seconds, and finish with the juice of half a lime.

Repeat for the second bowl. Serve with chilli fish sauce.

Chicken & sweetcorn soup

This is the sort of soup best suited to the lean, cruel months of January and February. So it's a bore that the very best sweetcorn is out of season. Still, use the imported stuff if it has sufficient sweetness. Or freeze a glut in the summer and autumn months. This is not the place for a stock cube: using my 5-hour stock will produce something that is rich, soothing and restorative.

Bring the stock to the boil in a large saucepan and simmer uncovered for 15 minutes, to reduce a little.

Add the corn kernels to the stock and cook for 2 minutes. Stir in the shredded chicken and simmer for a further 5 minutes, until cooked through. Add the spring onions and lemon juice and season to taste with salt, pepper and a dash of Tabasco. Serve.

{ SERVES 4 }

1.2 litres/2 pints dark chicken stock (see page 39)
2 corn ears, kernels stripped from the cobs
200 g/7 oz boneless cooked chicken (the best you can afford), shredded
2 spring onions, sliced
juice of ½ lemon
sea salt and freshly ground black pepper
Tabasco

My mother's roast chicken

{ SERVES 4 }

1 unwaxed lemon
1 x 1.8 kg/4 lb chicken (the best you can afford), rinsed inside and out with cold water and then drained
sea salt and freshly ground black pepper
about 75 g/3 oz butter, at room temperature

Gravy
200 ml/7 fl oz dry white wine
450 ml/16 fl oz chicken stock (a cube is fine)

My wife swore that if she heard me mention this dish one more time, she'd shove it where the sun don't beam. Well, words to that effect. Because this was such a staple of my youth, I roll it out any time anyone asks if my mother is a good cook – which is pretty much all of the time. She is, although she was always less bothered with the cakes, puddings and pies side of things: anything that requires exact measurements. Which was fine by us. All my sister and I really wanted was Findus Crispy Pancakes and Ice Magic chocolate sauce. Sadly, we had to seek those illicit pleasures elsewhere.

This is a classic recipe, cooked in the top right-hand oven of the Aga. I've adapted it for normal ovens. My mother insists that chopping off that dangly bit above the cavity and putting it on top of the bird improves the flavour. As it releases about a ton of schmaltz, or chicken fat, I'd agree. Buy the best chicken you can afford. Rather eat one decent free-range than four of those flabby imported beasts with all the depth of a puddle.

Preheat the oven to 220°C/425°F/Gas 7. Pierce the lemon with a small knife and 'shove it up the chicken's bottom'. Season the bird with salt and pepper, inside and out, then massage the butter all over it. Cook for 20 minutes, then turn the oven down to 180°C/350°F/Gas 4 and cook for a further 40 minutes. Poke a skewer into the thickest part of the thigh: the juices should be golden, not pink. If not, cook for a little longer, then retest. Let it rest for 15–20 minutes.

Meanwhile, for the gravy, spoon excess fat from the roasting tin, but leave a little in the tin. Put the tin over a high heat. When everything starts bubbling, deglaze with the white wine. Simmer while the alcohol cooks off, then add the stock, stirring all the time. Tip in any juices from the resting chicken. Boil to reduce a little, then strain through a sieve into a warm jug. Serve the chicken with the gravy.

Chicken & mushroom pie

Nothing beats a good pie when nights are long and credit short. I'm far too lazy to make my own puff pastry, especially when the supermarkets have decent ready-made stuff. Just ensure it's all-butter, as the pastry made with margarine is predictably nasty. When roasting a chicken for dinner, add another one to eat later. As ever, the better the chicken, the finer the taste and texture.

Melt 50 g/1¾ oz of the butter in a saucepan over a low heat, then stir in the flour (one of those small Wonder Whisks makes life much easier) and cook for about 2 minutes. Don't let it colour. Slowly add the hot stock until you have a thick sauce. Season, then add the mustard, lemon juice and a few dashes of Tabasco and leave to simmer for 2 minutes.

Sauté the onion and the fresh and soaked mushrooms in the remaining butter until soft. Add the wine, bring to the boil to cook off the alcohol, then add the mixture to the sauce, stirring over a medium heat for a couple of minutes. Add the chicken and herbs, then allow to cool.

Preheat the oven to 200°C/400°F/Gas 6. Put the chicken mixture into a 2 litre/3½ pint pie dish and brush the edge with a little beaten egg. Roll out the pastry on a lightly floured surface and lift onto the pie dish. Cut a couple of small vents in the pastry and press around the edges to seal well. Brush with beaten egg and bake for 30–35 minutes, or until golden brown.

{ SERVES 4–6 }

75 g/3 oz butter
50 g/1¾ oz plain flour, sifted, plus extra for rolling pastry
600 ml/20 fl oz hot chicken stock
sea salt and freshly ground black pepper
2 teaspoons Dijon mustard
juice of 1 lemon
Tabasco
1 large onion, finely chopped
225 g/8 oz button mushrooms, sliced
15 g/½ oz dried morels, soaked in warm water, drained and chopped (optional, as they are expensive but they do add some mycological magic)
150 ml/5 fl oz dry white wine
1 cold roasted chicken (the best you can afford), flesh stripped and cut into bite-sized pieces
1 tablespoon finely chopped tarragon
1 tablespoon finely chopped flat-leaf parsley
1 egg, beaten, to glaze
500 g/1 lb 2 oz all-butter puff pastry

{ Chicken stock }

Stock used to scare the hell out of me. Not literally. It never chased me through the woods with a bloody cleaver, or harangued me on the Second Coming of Christ. No, my fear of stock was purely practical. Unlike frying an egg, say, or making a curry, it seemed to involve vast, industrial vats overflowing with centuries of serious culinary know-how. I saw it as a professional process, mastered by moustachioed French chefs, their hands riddled with scars, their toques white and priapic. 'The foundation of French cuisine,' they'd mutter, in gutteral Gallic, before browning a few kilos of chicken wings in a world-weary way.

But one day, fed up with the impotent insipidity of the shop-bought versions, I gave it a go. I followed a recipe, probably by Nigel Slater, and managed to transform a couple of old carcasses, along with a few tired vegetables squatting in the bottom of my fridge, into a golden nectar, good enough to drink. I had created something wonderful from the drab, useless and everyday. Bless you, kitchen chemistry. You never cease to amaze. And so I became a maker of stock, a process every bit as soothing as it is satisfactory.

As the years have passed, so my stock recipe has evolved. Dark chicken stock is my liquid of choice, made from at least two carcasses (frozen leftovers from a roast chicken – when there are two foil-wrapped parcels in the deep freeze, it's time to make stock) and roasted wings. These wings, I reckon, are the secret weapons, although necks and hearts are grand, too. No liver though, as it adds an unpleasant bitter note. Very occasionally, towards the end of the winter, I might throw in a grouse that has lurked in the icy depths too long. Or a partridge carcass. The more flavour, the better, especially as the vast majority of my stock goes into either spicy, Thai-tinged broths or proper risottos that crave a serious savoury punch.

Although it can be a good way of using up carrots sulking in the depths of one's fridge, the fresher the vegetables, the better the stock will taste. Contrary to traditional knowledge, stock is *not* a rubbish dump for geriatric onions and rotten tomatoes, nor should it be left forever bubbling, as you throw in whatever seems fit. Tomatoes add sweetness, as do onions (keep their skin on for colour). Celery adds … well, celery is the most mysterious of vegetables. Raw, it's pretty dull and one-noted. Cooked down, it adds a sensual roundness that a stock cannot live without. A few parsley and coriander stalks add still more depth (I just freeze them after using the leaves), along with peppercorns and a brace of bay leaves.

Every cook will have his or her own version. Purists will go for bones alone,

Michelin-starred maestros might favour a very light stock, cooked for no more than an hour or two, so as not to overwhelm. But I'm an eater, not a saucier, and I want a lot of roasted chicken heft. So mine takes about 5 hours. At the meekest of simmers. I plunge my roasted carcasses and wings into cold water (and a big stockpot is a must; up there with a good knife and proper wok, it's a stalwart of my kitchen), bring to the boil, skim off the scum, then turn down the heat until it's just a flickering flame, add the vegetables, herbs and aromatics, and let it blip away. Just a blip, mind, not even a simmer. When the cooking time is up, taste, sieve and pour into jugs to cool. Let the dark sediment settle at the bottom, then pour off the clear liquid and use or freeze. It's ready for risotto.

For broth, I reduce it by about a third to intensify the flavour. To clarify further, there are endless clever ways with egg whites and mince. But I'm buggered if I know what they are. My stock is for cooking, slurping and sipping, so I don't lose too much sleep over a few minuscule and flavour-packed specks. This is cooking as therapy, a balm and salve. And you get a few litres of amber nectar at the end. Super stock, indeed.

A darkish, deeply flavoured chicken stock

{ **MAKES ABOUT 5 LITRES / 9 PINTS** }

2 cooked chicken carcasses, kept from roast chicken
8 chicken wings, roasted for 20 minutes at 220°C/450°F/Gas 7
chicken neck and heart (optional but preferable)
2 large tomatoes, quartered
2 large onions, quartered
2 large carrots, roughly chopped
3 celery stalks, roughly chopped (with leaves, if present)
handful of mixed parsley and coriander stalks
2 bay leaves
8 black peppercorns

Cut or tear up the carcasses into small pieces and put into a large stockpot, along with the wings and neck and heart if using. Cover with cold water (filtered is best; it sounds poncey, but it does make a difference to the flavour) and bring to the boil. Skim off any scum and turn down the heat.

Add the tomatoes, vegetables, herbs and peppercorns and cook for 5 hours, covered, over a flickering flame. You want blip blip, not bubble bubble.

Use a slotted spoon to discard all the meat and vegetables. Pour the liquid through a fine sieve into jugs. Leave it to sit and cool.

After an hour, most of the sediment will drop to the bottom of the jugs. Skim off excess fat – but leave some. Pour the stock into freezer bags, leaving the sediment behind.

A really good fish pie

{ SERVES 6 }

600 ml/20 fl oz full-fat milk
½ small onion, thinly sliced
6 black peppercorns
1 bay leaf
2 fresh parsley stalks
blade of mace
300 g/10½ oz undyed smoked haddock
115 g/4 oz cod fillets
150 ml/5 fl oz dry white wine
Tabasco
175 g/6 oz small cooked prawns, shelled
1 small pot (about 55 g/2 oz) potted shrimps
24 uncooked queen scallops, about 200 g/7 oz (optional)
big pinch of finely chopped flat-leaf parsley

For the mash

1.3 kg/3 lb Maris Piper potatoes, scrubbed
sea salt and freshly ground black pepper
6 tablespoons full-fat milk
50 g/1¾ oz butter, plus 25 g/1 oz to dot on top

There's no place for salmon in a proper fish pie. I'm sorry, but it's just not right. It's somehow too greasy, too lurid and too, well, salmony, to feel anything but ill at ease. It's not that I hate salmon. The wild stuff is a rare treat, rich and magnificent. And there are a couple of decent salmon farmers (Loch Duart, for one) that allow these once-great beasts space to swim and build up their muscles and fins. But the vast majority of farmed stuff is pap, pure and simple. Ruinous to the environment, and equally dull on the palate. Smoked haddock, on the other hand, is the backbone of this pie. Undyed, of course, alongside some good unsmoked fish, for contrast and balance. A few prawns add life, and queen scallops are a fine addition, too. Even a pot or two of potted shrimps. A good béchamel is essential, and a whisper of booze. But eggs are just gilding the lily. This pie is all about the fish.

To make the mash, put the potatoes in a big pan of salted water, bring to the boil, then simmer for 20–25 minutes, until a knife goes through with ease. Tip into a colander, let them cool down a little, then peel. Heat the milk and butter in a small saucepan until the butter melts, then mash the potatoes with the milk. Season.

Preheat the oven to 180°C/350°F/Gas 4. Put the milk, onion, peppercorns, bay leaf, parsley stalks and mace in a large shallow pan, heat to a simmer and then poach the smoked

{ CONTINUES OVERLEAF }

For the béchamel sauce
50 g/1¾ oz butter
50 g/1¾ oz plain flour
2 tablespoons double cream
white pepper

haddock and cod for 5–6 minutes, until the fish just flakes when pressed with a knife. Lift out the fish, remove the skin and any stray bones and set aside. Strain the milk through a sieve into a measuring jug; discard the flavourings. If necessary, add a little extra milk to make up to 600 ml/ 20 fl oz; set aside.

To make the béchamel sauce, melt the butter in a saucepan over a low heat, stir in the flour using a wooden spoon, and cook for 2–3 minutes; do not let it brown. Remove from the heat and slowly stir in the reserved milk until smooth. Add the cream and cook for 2–3 minutes, adding salt and white pepper to taste.

Add the wine to the béchamel and cook gently, stirring, for a further 2–3 minutes. Add a big dash of Tabasco. Add the fish, shellfish and chopped parsley and put into a pie dish.

Cover the fish mixture with the mash; using a fork, fluff up the top into small waves and dot with a little extra butter. Put in the oven for 20–30 minutes, until the top is golden.

Haddock Parker Bowles

{ SERVES 4 }

2 plum tomatoes
50 g/1¾ oz butter
4 x 175 g/6 oz undyed smoked haddock fillets, skinned
4 eggs

For the white wine sauce
2 large shallots, finely chopped
25 g/1 oz butter
175 ml/6 fl oz dry white wine
150 ml/5 fl oz fish stock
150 ml/5 fl oz double cream
juice of ½ lemon

For the mash
650 g/1 lb 7 oz Maris Piper potatoes, scrubbed
3 tablespoons full-fat milk
25 g/1 oz butter
sea salt and freshly ground black pepper
25 g/1 oz chives, chopped

My grandfather was a good cook, in a time when gentlemen were rarely seen in the kitchen. My father has a picture of him in his apron, looking very pukka. It was probably made on Savile Row. My uncle Simon carried on the family tradition with Green's, a proper English restaurant and oyster bar. It has the feeling of a St James's club, although the food is markedly superior. And Haddock Parker Bowles could be described as a signature dish. It's certainly never been off the menu since the first restaurant opened in St James's in 1982 (there's now another Green's in Cornhill, in the City). The current recipe is wonderful, but a little too cheffy for my tastes (in the cooking, not the eating). So I've pared it down a little, although the essence remains. Make the tomato concassé first, along with the sauce, which can be reheated. And poach the eggs just after you've made the mash.

First, make the tomato concassé. Pierce the tomatoes, then put them in a bowl of boiling water for 30 seconds. Run them under the cold tap. Peel, cut into quarters, remove the seeds and cut the flesh into small dice.

To make the sauce, sweat the shallots in the butter over a low–medium heat until soft and just turning golden. Combine the white wine and stock and use to deglaze the pan, then reduce slowly until lightly syrupy. Add the cream and reduce until the sauce coats the back of a spoon.

{ CONTINUES OVERLEAF }

Strain through a sieve, then add the lemon juice. Season and keep warm.

Make the mash. Put the potatoes in a big pan of salted water, bring to the boil, then simmer for 20–25 minutes, until a knife goes through with ease. Tip them into a colander, let them cool a little, then peel. Heat the milk and butter in a saucepan until the butter melts, then mash the potatoes with the milk. Season, mix with the chives and keep warm.

For the fish, melt the butter in a large frying pan over a medium heat and fry the haddock fillets for about 8 minutes, until brown and the fish flakes easily when pressed with a knife, turning halfway through cooking. Allow to rest.

Poach the eggs (see my method on page 51), then drain.

To serve, put the chive mash on 4 warmed plates, top with haddock and a poached egg. Pour the sauce around the fish, and sprinkle with the tomato concassé.

Goujons of sole, haddock or even pollack (if you must)

{ SERVES 4 }

300 g/10½ oz white bread, a couple of days old, no crusts
200 g/7 oz plain flour
sea salt and freshly ground black pepper
4 eggs, beaten
1 kg/2 lb 4 oz sole, cod, haddock, plaice, pollack, filleted, skinned and cut into strips somewhere between the size of your small and ring fingers
6 tablespoons olive oil
3 lemons, cut into wedges

For the pea purée
900 g/2 lb frozen petit pois
25 g/1 oz salted butter
a few sprigs of mint
splash of hot chicken stock

A goujon is a fish finger with a French accent and Chanel bag. They're incredibly easy to make and it's a lunch that the children love as much as we do. Sole is expensive, but perfect. If buying haddock, make sure it's sustainably caught – the same with cod and plaice. Rather than have me wagging my finger at you, check out the Marine Stewardship Council website to see which fish you can and can't eat (www.msc.org). Some people suggest pollack. But there's a reason we haven't eaten this fish for years … it's deadly dull. As my friend Matthew Fort would say, 'Bollocks to pollacks.'

Tear the bread into small pieces and blitz in a food processor to make crumbs, then put them on a plate. Mix the flour with a little salt and pepper and lay out on another plate. Put the eggs in a shallow dish.

Using one hand (this stops both hands getting clagged up), dip the fish strips into the flour, then egg, then breadcrumbs, shaking off any excess at each stage.

Fry the fish in batches in a couple of tablespoons of olive oil, over a medium–high heat, until crisp and golden, then drain on kitchen paper. Keep hot while cooking the rest.

For the pea purée, cook the peas in a saucepan of boiling water for 4–5 minutes, then drain. Put them into a blender, add the butter and mint and blend, adding hot chicken stock to thin it out as needed (I like it to be quite thick, so you can use the goujons as golden spoons). Season and serve with the goujons and wedges of lemon.

Baked potatoes with caviar

{ SERVES 4 }

4 small baking potatoes – use a floury type such as Maris Piper
2 tablespoons soured cream
50–60 g/about 2 oz unsalted butter
125 g/4 oz caviar (ideally Royal Belgian from www.kingsfinefoods.co.uk)

OK, so this is a rare treat. And with wild sturgeon in perilous decline, a ruinously expensive one, too. But there is some first-class farmed caviar out there, miles removed from that muddy muck from years gone by. I once went to a caviar tasting with Laura King, the real expert on all matters ovoid and salted. With me was chef Rowley Leigh and food writer Bill Knott. She opened a vast 5 kg/11 lb tin of wild beluga (the biggest of the caviar eggs, the rarest and most expensive, though in my view no better or worse than oscietra, just different). We all took polite nibbles, but for Bill, the temptation was too much. When Laura turned her back, he dug deep and emerged with a mass of these oily black eggs piled atop his mother-of-pearl spoon. A huge gash now marked the previously pristine surface, christened by Laura as the Knott Trench.

As a deeply greedy person, and a caviar freak, I'd rather eat a glut or nothing at all. The contrast of cool eggs and hot, creamy potato is one of the best in the world. It'll probably cost you the same as dinner for two at Le Gavroche. In its own way, and eaten rarely, it's every bit as good.

Preheat the oven to 220°C/425°F/Gas 7. Bake the potatoes for about 45 minutes, until crisp and soft inside.

Carefully cut open the potatoes and scoop the insides into a bowl. Add the soured cream and butter, mix until the butter melts, then spoon back into the potatoes.

Heap with caviar and eat at once.

Potted shrimps

There are many claimants to the crustacean throne, with various lobsters and crabs elbowing their way into our affections. But the modest brown shrimp, *Crangon crangon*, is a definite contender. The only prawn we call a shrimp (unlike the Americans, who call all prawns shrimp), it's small and intensely sweet. The best in the world come from Morecambe Bay in Lancashire. Potting is one of those old British techniques that has fallen by the wayside, but before the invention of refrigeration, covering cooked beef, ham, crab or lobster with a layer of butter didn't just add to the flavour, it preserved, too. Serve cold with slices of brown bread and butter, or hot on good toast.

{ SERVES 6 }

175 g/6 oz unsalted butter
1 teaspoon ground black pepper
½ teaspoon ground cayenne pepper
½ teaspoon ground mace
1 small bay leaf
450 g/1 lb peeled brown shrimps
sea salt
brown bread, sliced, to serve
3 lemons, cut into wedges, to serve

In a saucepan over a medium–low heat, melt the butter, then add the black pepper, cayenne pepper, mace and bay leaf. Throw in the shrimps and stir to coat. Cook for a couple of minutes until brown and cooked, then remove from the heat and leave until just warm. Remove the bay leaf and check the seasoning.

Divide the shrimp mixture among 6 ramekins and season with a little salt. The butter should cover the shrimps. Put the mixture into the fridge and chill until set.

Toast the brown bread; serve with the potted shrimps and a wedge of lemon.

{ Eggs }

I once spent an entire week going to work on a diet of eggs. Eggs and pretty much nothing else. I was allowed butter or oil to cook them in, as well as herbs, chillies, onions and any other secondary ingredient deemed appropriate to the matter in hand. A little cheese or ham could creep in for an omelette, say, but mustn't become the star of the show. Bacon was a no-no, despite my protestations (fried eggs cry out for crisp shavings of smoked, cured pork), and mayonnaise *verboten*. This ovoid diet wasn't done for pleasure, I hasten to add, nor culinary curiosity. Nope, it was a commissioned piece for the *Mail on Sunday* in reaction to news of the Charles Saatchi diet. The great advertising guru and contemporary art collector had lost huge amounts of weight on a similar diet, despite being married to Nigella Lawson. A triumph of the will, if I ever heard one. And I was to sample a mere seven days.

The first day was fine. Boiled egg for breakfast, fried egg sandwich for lunch, masala scrambled eggs for dinner. The next day started with a poached pair on toast, and a craving for anything, anything but egg. I walked past sausage shops and curry houses, burger joints and brasseries, longing for a change. Lunch was another omelette, eaten resentfully. And by dinner, my baked egg became a figure of hate. Five more long, dreary and frustrating days followed. My digestion shut up shop, my burps became toxic … I became toxic. Damn you, eggs. Once the experiment was over, I didn't touch another for at least a month.

Despite the occasional blip, though, I love eggs, worship their curves, adore them in their every form. Fried in butter and plonked between two slices of cheap white bread or whisked into still more butter to make hollandaise sauce. Boiled with soldiers, baked with ham, coddled, scrambled and poached. Even raw, draped over steak tartare. They're the ultimate convenience food, perfectly packaged and endlessly versatile. French cuisine would be lost without them. Actually, most of mankind would have problems making do without them.

Eggs cover every base, from economy food (tortilla, say) to comfort (baked eggs), home cooking (scrambled eggs) to haute cuisine (*oeufs à la neige*). Hen eggs might be our staple, but duck and goose eggs have a special richness all of their own. Don't even get me started on eggs from fish.

But too often we forget the basics. There was uproar when Delia started her *How to Cook* with boiling an egg. 'Outrage!' cried the snobs. 'Off with her head!' bellowed the buffoons. Surely, they moaned, everyone knew how to boil an egg? Well, they don't. It's not difficult, but there are a few factors to take into account. How fresh is the egg (particularly important when it comes to poached eggs), how big, and exactly how hard do you like your white? I have no problem with it being a little 'spermy', but my wife cannot bear the sight of uncooked albumen. So while not attempting to teach my grandmother to, *ahem*, suck eggs, these recipes all work for me.

There is much debate about how to poach eggs. You need a shallow saucepan with a lid. Bring salted water to the boil in the pan. Break the eggs into ramekins (the fresher the eggs, the better). Turn off the heat, then drop in the eggs. Leave them for 3 minutes, then lift out with a slotted spoon and drain on kitchen paper.

As with chicken and pigs, I do believe free-range eggs are superior to those produced by barn-reared chickens (if it doesn't say 'organic' or 'free-range', assume the worst). The difference in taste is huge. Dull, insipid and watery, eggs from barn-reared chickens are the end product of a wretched life. And they are a waste of money, too. Rather eat one decent egg than two second-rate ones.

Fresh eggs are best and if you're lucky enough to have chickens, then yee-ha: you can date the eggs with easy precision. In fact, the eggs from my father's chickens are the best I've ever tasted. His birds eat better than we do, with veggie scraps and grit to keep the shells hard. But buy the freshest you can find (difficult in a supermarket). A good test is to drop an egg in a glass of water (not convenient for the aisles of Asda or Sainsbury's, I know). If it drops to the bottom, it's fresh. The further it floats towards the surface, the older it is. If it bobs gaily on the top, bin it.

Chorizo scrambled eggs

{ SERVES 4 }

olive oil, for frying

200 g/7 oz soft picante chorizo, sliced into 1 cm/½ inch thick pieces

4 tablespoons diced stale white bread

8 eggs, beaten

sea salt and freshly ground pepper

½ teaspoon dried red chilli flakes

2 tablespoons roughly chopped flat-leaf parsley

fried potatoes, to serve (optional)

This is all about texture and contrast. Frazzled chorizo, crisp bread and wobbling, just set egg. A Spanish classic.

Heat a dash of olive oil in a frying pan and fry the chorizo over a medium–high heat until it begins to crisp. Add the diced bread and fry, stirring from time to time, until brown.

Stir in the eggs, season and add the chilli. Turn the heat down to extremely low and scramble the eggs very slowly for 15–20 minutes, stirring all the time, until soft and creamy. Sprinkle with chopped parsley and serve with fried potatoes if you wish.

Baked eggs

{ SERVES 2 }

a little chopped ham or cooked asparagus (optional)
4 eggs
2–3 tablespoons double cream
4 teaspoons butter
sea salt and freshly ground black pepper
hot toast, to serve

This is one of my mother's 'signature' dishes, although she'd be perplexed as to what a 'signature' dish is. When we used to arrive home, late, from holiday, the house would be cold and dark, the fridge bare. But my sister and I would collect the eggs, and my mother would break them into ramekins, splosh in a little cream from the top of the milk bottle and dot with butter.

Preheat the oven to 180°C/350°F/Gas 4.

If using ham or asparagus, divide this between 2 ramekins. Break the eggs into the ramekins, then add the cream, butter, salt and pepper.

Put into a small roasting pan and pour in some just-boiled water to come halfway up the sides of the ramekins. Bake for 7–10 minutes, until the yolk is wobbling and the white just set. Serve with toast.

Fried eggs

Ah, the great dilemma – butter or goose fat? The latter is better for a serious treat, but the former should be the default option. Olive oil is fine, but it does seem a wasted opportunity. Butter and egg are the closest of friends.

Break the egg into a ramekin. Heat a small frying pan over a medium heat, add the butter and heat until it is just bubbling. Slip in the egg.

Tidy up any edges (the older the egg is, the more the white will sprawl across the pan) and keep basting the egg using a spoon. Pay close attention to the yolk, but don't over-baste.

Once the yolk takes on an opaque sheen, the white is set and the edges a touch frilly (up to 3 minutes, depending on size), remove with a spatula onto a piece of kitchen paper. Season and serve.

{ SERVES 1 }

1 egg
25 g/1 oz salted butter
sea salt and freshly ground black pepper

Tortilla

{ **SERVES 4** }

4 tablespoons olive oil
2 onions, ideally Spanish yellow, thinly sliced
2 waxy potatoes, such as Charlotte, peeled and cut into small dice
pinch of crushed chillies
8 eggs, beaten
sea salt and freshly ground black pepper

There are two important factors to the perfect tortilla. First, the right-sized pan is crucial. You need a small frying pan, about 15 cm/6 inches in diameter. As these Spanish potato and onion omelettes are perfect for everything from breakfast to picnics, it's well worth the investment. The second lies in the caramelisation of the onions… low and slow, so that golden hue is teased out, adding immeasurable depth to the flavour. You want a gently oozing centre, too.

Heat half the oil in a large frying pan, add the onions and cook over a low heat for at least 30 minutes, until soft and golden. Add the potatoes and chillies, increase the heat a little and cook for another 20 minutes, until the potatoes are golden, with a hint of crust. Tip everything into a bowl and leave to cool slightly.

When cool, add the beaten eggs, season and mix. Heat the remaining olive oil in a 15 cm/6 inch frying pan until hot, then add the egg and potato mixture and cook for 4 minutes, using a spatula to run around the edge.

When the bottom of the omelette is firm, flip it out of the pan onto a plate, put the pan back on the heat and slip in the omelette, uncooked side down. Cook for a further 3–4 minutes, until nearly set, then turn out and cut into 4 pieces.

Huevos rancheros

You'll find this classic breakfast dish all over Mexico and the southwestern USA, and it ranks up alongside bacon and eggs as the royalty of the breakfast boys. It's the perfect early morning heart-starter, the sauce possessing just enough kick to jolt the senses into action, while that yolk softens everything. You can cook the sauce in advance, to make things easier. And do try to get proper corn tortillas (available from www.coolchile.co.uk), as that maize tang is truly the soul of Mexican food. You can use those El Paso versions from the supermarket – but they just don't taste the same.

{ SERVES 2 }

500 g/1 lb 2 oz tomatoes
groundnut oil, for frying
1–3 fresh jalapeño peppers, finely chopped
sea salt and freshly ground black pepper
pinch of caster sugar
2 small corn tortillas
2 eggs

Pierce the tomatoes, then put them in a bowl of boiling water for 30 seconds. Run them under the cold tap. Peel, cut into quarters, remove and discard the seeds and then finely chop the flesh.

Heat 1–2 tablespoons oil in a heavy-based frying pan, add the tomatoes and jalapeños and cook over a low heat for about 25 minutes, or until the tomatoes are reduced to a thick sauce. Season to taste with salt, pepper and a pinch of sugar.

In another frying pan, heat a little oil and fry the tortillas for a few seconds on each side, to soften. Drain on kitchen paper, wrap in foil and keep warm.

Fry the eggs in the same pan, adding more oil if needed, until the whites are set but the yolks are still runny.

To serve, put a warm tortilla on each plate, top with a fried egg and then spoon on some tomato sauce, leaving the yolk exposed.

'Gegs (9–4)'*

{ SERVES 2 }

* Scrambled eggs

6 eggs
sea salt and freshly ground
  black pepper
50–60 g/about 2 oz salted butter
hot toast, to serve

This is a beautiful cryptic-crossword clue. Slow and low is the key. You want fat, creamy curds, rather than rubbery globules of overcooked protein. The only way to guarantee this is to cook over the lowest possible heat. Use a heat diffuser if you have one. If not, go to the lowest flame and remove the pan from the heat if it gets too hot. There's no need for milk or cream; just good, fresh eggs, butter, salt and pepper.

Break the eggs into a bowl, add 1 teaspoon of water, a pinch of salt and a twist of pepper and mix with a fork. Don't beat the hell out of them, just do enough for them to get to know each other better.

Heat the butter in a saucepan until it just about melts. Pour in the eggs and stir over the lowest possible heat. You don't want anything to happen for at least 5–7 minutes. Keep stirring, stretching those curds. Slowly, very slowly, the eggs will start to firm up. If it happens too quickly, remove the pan from the heat. After 15–20 minutes, they will be ready. Serve on hot toast.

Variation
Finely chop a small onion and a red chilli, then sizzle in half the butter until soft; allow to cool slightly. Add the remaining butter and melt, then add the eggs mixed with 1 teaspoon water and seasoning and cook as above. Two minutes before it is ready, add 1 skinned, deseeded and finely chopped tomato and a handful of finely chopped fresh coriander.

Mayonnaise

Everyone used to tell me how easy mayonnaise was to make. I'd try it, split the bugger and give up for another few years. But then came the breakthrough. Some patient chef explained that, aside from making sure the eggs are at room temperature, it's all about the initial emulsion of oil and yolk. Keep the faith and add the oil a drop at a time, until you have that thick base. After that you can add the oil in a thin stream. The rest is easy. Use a bowl with a narrow base and perch it on a tea towel to prevent slipping.

{ MAKES ABOUT 300 ML/½ PINT }

2 egg yolks, at room temperature
1 teaspoon Dijon mustard
sea salt and freshly ground
   black pepper
225 ml/8 fl oz sunflower oil
75 ml/3½ fl oz extra-virgin
   olive oil
big squeeze of lemon juice

Put the yolks, mustard, salt and pepper in a bowl and whisk together for a good minute. The mustard helps the emulsion and the salt helps thicken.

Add a tiny drop of the sunflower oil and whisk hard. Once amalgamated, add a drop more and repeat. Keep doing this until the mixture starts to thicken, then you can get a bit more free with the pouring. But keep whisking and make sure the mixture emulsifies before you add more oil. Add the rest of the sunflower oil in a steady stream, whisking all the time, then slowly pour in the olive oil and continue to whisk. Once all the oil is used, taste and adjust the seasoning, add the lemon juice and whisk again. If it's too thick, whisk in a couple of teaspoons of warm water.

French onion soup

{ SERVES 8–10 }

300 g/10½ oz butter
8 large Spanish onions, sliced as thin as possible (a mandolin is perfect for this)
salt and freshly ground black pepper
½ tablespoon plain flour
150 ml/5 fl oz dry white wine (or a glug of Port if you want a slightly sweeter, richer note)
4 tablespoons sherry vinegar or red wine vinegar
a few sprigs of thyme
2 litres/3½ pints hot beef or dark brown chicken stock (see page 39)
1 baguette, cut into thin slices
2–3 tablespoons olive oil
175–200 g/6–7 oz Gruyère, Emmental or Beaufort cheese, grated

This is one of those dishes for which you really have to make your own stock. Or buy some good stuff from the butcher. There's nowhere for bad ingredients to hide. The onions are easy enough to cook (although be prepared to keep a constant eye on them for up to 3 hours … this requires concentration rather than any real skill), but good stock provides the depth. My wife sometimes complains that the 3-hour caramelised onions are a little too sweet. She has a point: this is a dish to be served in starter-sized portions, otherwise it can overwhelm. As it takes so long, it makes sense to make a big batch. Any leftovers can be frozen for another night.

Melt the butter in a heavy saucepan over a medium–high heat and add the onions and a big pinch of salt. Once they are bubbling away, turn the heat right down to very low and cook for 2–3 hours. Have faith. They'll start off milky and drab, but check and stir every 10 or so minutes and try not to let them burn at all. As the time passes, they'll take on a deep golden hue.

Stir in the flour, then deglaze the pan with the wine and vinegar. Add the thyme, hot stock and black pepper, and cook gently for around 1 hour.

Meanwhile, preheat the oven to 180°C/350°F/Gas 4. Just before serving, put the baguette slices on a baking sheet, sprinkle with olive oil and salt and bake until crisp. Preheat the grill to high. Cover the baguette slices with cheese. Whack them under the grill until just burnished and bubbling. Ladle the soup into bowls and serve with the cheesy baguette.

Cauliflower cheese

{ SERVES 4 }

1 large cauliflower
sea salt
500 ml/18 fl oz full-fat milk
1 small onion, finely chopped
2 cloves
1 bay leaf
50 g/1¾ oz butter
50 g/1¾ oz plain flour
200 g/7 oz good strong
   Cheddar, grated
pinch of freshly grated nutmeg
¼ teaspoon cayenne pepper
1 teaspoon English
   mustard powder

For the tomato salad
2 tomatoes
sea salt and freshly ground
   black pepper
½ red onion, thinly sliced
extra-virgin olive oil,
   for drizzling
red wine vinegar, for sprinkling

I used to dread this as a child at school. Actually, I dreaded all school food, save those strange reconstituted pork ribs, garish red and shaped like a chocolate bar. Those were OK. But the cauliflower cheese… ugh. An overcooked, watery mass drowning in a bland white sauce thick with uncooked flour and the meanest pinch of sweaty block Cheddar. The sauce would congeal on the plate, with a wretched, translucent moat around it. This is the exact opposite: a generous, hearty and deeply-flavoured delight with a subtle tang of heat. The tomato salad offers a pert, sharp foil to all that dairy glory. It's an unlikely but perfect partner.

Remove and discard the green leaves from the cauliflower, then break into even-sized florets. Cook in a pan of salted boiling water for 8–10 minutes, or until nearly tender. Drain and lay out on a folded tea towel to absorb excess moisture.

Put the milk in a saucepan, add the onion, cloves and bay leaf and bring to a simmer. Cook for 1–2 minutes, then cover and remove from the heat. Set aside to infuse for 10 minutes, then strain the milk through a sieve into a jug.

In another saucepan, melt the butter over a low heat and stir in the flour, making sure there are no lumps in the mixture. Cook, stirring, for a few minutes, then remove from the heat.

Pour in the milk, whisking vigorously until smooth and well combined. Return the pan to a low heat and, using a wooden spoon, stir until the sauce thickens enough to coat the back of the spoon. Leave to cook for a further 2–3 minutes over the lowest heat. Preheat the oven to 190°C/375°F/Gas 5.

Add three-quarters of the cheese to the sauce and stir until it melts. Season with nutmeg, cayenne, mustard powder and sea salt. Arrange the cauliflower in a shallow ovenproof dish, pour over the hot sauce and sprinkle with the remaining cheese. Bake for 20 minutes, until the cheese is golden and the sauce is bubbling.

Meanwhile, for the salad, slice the tomatoes, place them in a serving dish and season. Add the red onion, then drizzle with the olive oil and sprinkle lightly with the red wine vinegar. Serve alongside the cauliflower cheese.

Porcini risotto

{ SERVES 4 }

50 g/1¾ oz butter, plus 25 g/1 oz cut into small cubes and kept in the fridge
1 small onion, very finely chopped
300 g/10½ oz carnaroli or arborio rice (or *vialone nano*, although this is more traditionally used for seafood risottos)
200 ml/7 fl oz dry white wine
25 g/1 oz dried porcini mushrooms, soaked in boiling water to cover for 25 minutes, then chopped
1 litre/1¾ pints good chicken stock (see page 39), kept at a rolling boil
25 g/1 oz Parmesan, finely grated
sea salt and freshly ground black pepper

Risotto does require a little patience, but no superhuman culinary technique. If you can soften an onion and stir, you'll be fine. I was taught how to make it by the great Antonio Carluccio, fag in one hand and glass of red in the other. Occasionally, he removed one or the other and gave the pot a stir. I'm also indebted to Giorgio Locatelli, whose recipe I've sort of adapted below. (If 'adapted' is the right word; the recipes for risotto vary little from book to book.)

It's a very meditative process, with Planet Rock riffing in the background, and a glass of wine close at hand. In that ghastly therapy speak, 'me time.' As ever, try to get all your prep done before you start cooking: the butter cubed and put in the fridge, the cheese grated and the mushrooms soaked. If you're feeling massively cashed up and you're making this between about November and early January, grate fresh white Alba truffle over the top. This beauty is all about the scent – deep, musty and slightly filthy – rather than the flavour.

Heat the butter in a large, heavy-bottomed saucepan over a low heat. Add the onion and cook to soften for about 10 minutes, stirring from time to time. Add the rice and cook, stirring, for about 5 minutes, until it is white and glistening. Add the wine and cook off the alcohol for a couple of minutes. Add the mushrooms and soaking liquid.

Add a ladle of hot stock and cook over a medium–high heat, stirring almost constantly, until the liquid is absorbed. Repeat again and again, only adding more stock when the rice has soaked up the last lot. After 20–25 minutes the rice should be soft yet firm, with a slight grain of crunch in the middle. Every grain should be separately definable in the mouth, yet surge together as one in the pan. Take off the heat and leave to sit for a minute. Throw in the cold butter cubes and beat the hell out of the risotto with a wooden spoon, shaking the pan until all the butter is incorporated. Add the Parmesan and do the same. Season. Serve at once.

Lemon risotto

'Oh God,' I thought, when I heard this was appearing for lunch. It was our first day at a villa in Sicily, and the first thing we tried from our Tunisian cook, Naima. Lemon risotto sounded all wrong: both over-sweet and cloying. What appeared was a dish so perfect that we ate in stunned silence. That the rice was cooked perfectly was a given (she was a magical cook), but the lemon just sharpened the edges, lifted the dish up, while a touch of chilli gave heat. After devouring a few platefuls, I tried to write down the recipe. Naima was secretive at first, but did admit she used vegetable rather than chicken stock. How the hell could she get that much flavour from mere vegetable stock? Anyway, as the fortnight progressed, we all fell in love with Naima and her cooking. She was a master, peerless. I never did get the exact recipe, but this comes close, gleaned from many a furtive trip into the kitchen as she was knocking it up.

Heat the olive oil and 25 g/1 oz butter in a large, heavy-bottomed saucepan over a medium heat. Add the onion, carrots and celery and cook to soften for about 10 minutes, stirring from time to time. Add the rice and cook, stirring, until it is white and glistening – 4–5 minutes. Add the brandy and cook off the alcohol for a couple of minutes.

Add a ladle of hot stock and cook over a medium–high heat, stirring almost constantly, until all the liquid is absorbed. Repeat again and again, only adding more stock when the rice has soaked up the last lot. After about 20–25 minutes the rice should be soft yet firm, with a slight grain of crunch in the middle. Every grain should be separately definable in the mouth, yet somehow surge together as one in the pan.

Add the lemon zest and mix well. Take off the heat and leave to sit for a minute. Add the lemon juice, cold butter and Parmesan, beating hard and banging the pot around. Season and serve with more Parmesan.

{ SERVES 4 }

2 tablespoons olive oil

25 g/1 oz butter, plus 25 g/1 oz cut into small cubes and kept in the fridge

1 onion, finely chopped

2 carrots, finely chopped

2 celery stalks, finely chopped

300 g/10½ oz carnaroli or arborio rice (or *vialone nano*, although this is more traditionally used for seafood risottos)

125 ml/4 fl oz brandy

1 litre/1¾ pints fresh vegetable or chicken stock, kept at a rolling boil

juice and finely grated zest of 1 unwaxed lemon

25 g/1 oz Parmesan, finely grated, plus extra to serve

sea salt and freshly ground black pepper

Triple-cooked chips

{ SERVES 4 }

1.25 kg/2 lb 12 oz floury potatoes, peeled
1 litre/1¾ pints groundnut oil
1 litre/1¾ pints beef dripping or rendered animal fat (optional)
sea salt

I won't lie. Good chips are a shag to make. They involve three different stages and a quantity of boiling-hot oil. Not a problem in itself (although I still shiver when remembering those government adverts of my youth, where some poor, unsuspecting fool would throw water on their deep-fat fryer ... with predictably horrific results), but cooking chips does tend to make the house reek of fat. My wife actually bans me from doing it inside. So I have to sit outside, frying away al fresco.

As with roast potatoes, the choice of potato is paramount. You want a floury or mealy variety because they concentrate a greater amount of dry starch in their cells. During the cooking process, these cells puff and separate, producing the dry, fluffy texture that is so essential. I like a Maris Piper or King Edward, but the likes of Golden Wonder, Croft or Idaho are equally well suited. As for the frying oil, nothing beats decent beef dripping for the third cooking. It reaches a high heat without smoking and adds the most wonderful flavour. Chip masters in the north of England have long sworn by it. Groundnut oil is an acceptable alternative, but you do miss out on that extra meaty edge.

The two-stage frying method produces decent chips: a lower heat to cook the centre, followed by a higher one to crisp it all up. But better still is Heston Blumenthal's method. He's not only an incredible cook, but a gentleman, too. Anyway, he takes the three-times-cooked approach and it's excellent. In fact, triple-cooked chips are now ubiquitous in gastro-pubs across the land. It all started with Heston. I've adapted the recipe a little for added ease.

Wash the potatoes and cut into rectangular blocks, then into chips, 1 cm/½ inch thick.

Put the chips into a bowl of cold water for 10 minutes, changing the water twice to rinse off some of the starch. Drain well.

Bring a big pot of water to the boil and add the chips. Bring back to the boil and simmer gently (do not boil hard) for 4–5 minutes, until almost cooked. Using a slotted spoon, lift the chips out of the water and place on a cooling rack over a roasting tin. Allow to steam dry and, when cool, place in the fridge for 20 minutes.

In a deep-fat fryer, heat the groundnut oil to 130°C/270°F and plunge in the chips. After a while, they will take on a drier appearance. Do not let them brown at all. This takes about 5–8 minutes. Drain, let them cool, then put them back in the fridge for 20 minutes.

For the second frying stage, heat the rendered fat or dripping (or reheat the groundnut oil if you must) to 180°C/350°F in a deep-fat fryer. Plunge in the chips and cook until golden brown. This takes 8–10 minutes. Be patient in order to obtain a really crisp chip. Drain and season with salt. Serve immediately.

Roast potatoes

{ SERVES 6 }

1.3 kg/3 lb floury
  potatoes, peeled
sea salt
about 6 tablespoons goose fat
  or duck fat

Here's a subject to get everyone all aquiver. On the one hand, there are those who claim they cannot make a decent roast potato, whatever method they use. On the other, there are people who decree that their's is the only way. I sit somewhere in the middle. The two main points are these: for proper, fluffy-centred beauties with a crisp, burnished crust, you need floury potatoes such as King Edward, Romano or Desiree. The waxy varieties are quite unsuited to the task. You also need to roughen up the edges after boiling, but before roasting. This gives that crunchy edge. As to fat, everyone will tell you different: lard/dripping/olive oil/goose fat/duck fat. I use the last two. They have a high burning point (i.e. they don't burn and get bitter in the oven) and a great flavour.

Preheat the oven to 220°C/425°F/Gas 7. Cut the potatoes into irregular, but same size-ish shapes (uniformity is boring – no one wants identical potatoes – rather some big, some slightly smaller and very crunchy, with lots of those bits you scrape from the pan).

Throw them into a big saucepan and fill with water, adding a little salt. Bring to the boil and simmer for about 10 minutes, until the outsides are a little fluffy. A knife should pass easily through the cooked potato. Chef Rowley Leigh once gave me a fine bit of advice: 'Boil them as long as you dare.' You obviously don't want to end up with potato broth, but a few errant scraps are always welcome. Drain and leave to steam dry for about 10–15 minutes.

Once the potatoes are dryish, give the strainer a good old rattle, so the edges thump together and the exteriors roughen up. Put the fat in a roasting tin and heat in the oven for 5 minutes.

When the fat is sizzling and shimmering, remove the tin from the oven, chuck in the potatoes and, using a spoon, roll them about so every surface is covered in hot fat. Put into the oven and leave for 30 minutes. Have faith. Then take out and turn and cook for another 20 minutes. By now you can start treating each potato as an individual, turning as need be. They should be done within the hour, but instead of worrying about what the recipe says, just try them. Then you'll know for sure. Season with salt and serve immediately.

Aligot

{ SERVES 4 }

1 kg/2 lb 4 oz small–medium floury potatoes, such as King Edward
sea salt and freshly ground black pepper
2 large cloves garlic
125 ml/4 fl oz double cream
60 g/2¼ oz unsalted butter
300 g/10½ oz *tomme de Cantal* cheese, cut into very thin slices, or grated Caerphilly or Lancashire
hot milk, for mixing, if needed

Mashed potato and cheese. Whipped together. There's no doubting its primal allure. You do really need *tomme de Cantal* for this recipe, a soft, young white French cheese. You could substitute grated Caerphilly or a Lancashire (Mrs Kirkham's is the best), but then it would be cheesy mashed potato rather than *Aligot*. Which is no bad thing, either.

Boil the potatoes in their skins until tender: about 15–25 minutes, depending on size. Remove the skins and push the potato flesh through a sieve to give a dry purée. Season to taste with salt and pepper.

In a small bowl, crush the garlic with a little salt to soften.

Put the cream and butter in a heavy saucepan and heat until the butter melts. Add the potato and stir until thoroughly combined. Add the garlic. Stir in the cheese all at once, and beat vigorously until the mixture becomes smooth and elastic. It should pull into bubblegum-like strings when you lift the spoon: if the mixture is too stiff, add a little hot milk. Serve immediately.

Sprouts in stock

Brussels sprouts are more sinned against than sinning. It's often the memories of school food that taint these magnificent vegetables. Cooked to buggery, until soggy and sulphurous, they're foul. Treated with respect, though, they transform from dowdy lump into fresh-faced beauty. This recipe is quick, easy and guaranteed to transform the most dyed-in-the-wool sprout abuser to instant obsessive.

Heat the butter in a frying pan until foaming, then add the sprouts and cook gently for 5 minutes.

Add the hot stock, enough to cover the sprouts to not quite halfway, and the thyme, and cook for another 5 minutes, until it forms a sort of thin glaze on the vegetables. Add a shake of Tabasco, a squeeze of lemon juice, and salt and pepper to taste. Serve at once.

{ SERVES 4 }

25 g/1 oz butter

500 g/1 lb 12 oz Brussels sprouts, outer leaves removed, cut into 5 mm/¼-inch-thick rounds

250 ml/9 fl oz hot chicken stock (cube OK, fresh better)

big pinch of thyme leaves

Tabasco

juice of ½ lemon

sea salt and freshly ground black pepper

Sticky toffee pudding

{ SERVES 6 }

55 g/2 oz unsalted butter, softened, plus extra to butter the dish
175 g/6 oz dates, chopped
1 teaspoon bicarbonate of soda
175 g/6 oz caster sugar
2 eggs
175 g/6 oz self-raising flour
1 teaspoon vanilla extract
vanilla ice cream, to serve

For the sauce
300 ml/½ pint double cream
55 g/2 oz demerara sugar
1 dessertspoon black treacle

Not so long ago, I imagined this pudding as an old English classic (well, at least dating back to the time when sugar made it to our shores), devoured by Tristram Shandy, Daniel Deronda and David Copperfield in his dotage. Yet this is a relatively recent invention. Despite claims to the contrary, STP was not first conjured up by The Village Shop in Cartmel – although this is one of the best you can buy. But, according to Jane Grigson, by Francis Coulson of Sharrow Bay on Ullswater in the Lake District. There, the story goes, he came up with the original recipe that has been copied ever since. Even this, though, is open to conjecture. Chef Simon Hopkinson recalls Coulson's admission, over a typically splendid dinner, that 'There was this sweet woman in Lancashire … and such a lovely cook … Marvellous puddings! And, well, yes … there might have been a recipe published somewhere … But mine is much better, and we call our updated version the 'Icky-Sticky Toffee Sponge' to avoid any confusion!'

So perhaps the original recipe came from a Mrs Martin. A few years later, her son, Piers, contacted Simon to relay the origins of his mother's dish. Far from being some great national pudding, she actually got her recipe from a Canadian friend. The horror! Still, the British have quickly made it their own and the debate as to its roots detracts nothing from the utter beauty of this pudding. Don't scrimp on the sauce, and please: no nuts or slivers of peel, no chunks of chocolate or glugs of brandy. Sticky Toffee Pudding needs no embellishments. This is certainly not my take on the recipe. Just the original recipe, in all its glory. Don't mess with perfection.

{ **CONTINUES OVERLEAF** }

Preheat the oven to 180°C/350°F/Gas 4. Butter a baking tin about 20 x 13 cm/8 x 5 inches.

Boil the dates in 300 ml/½ pint water until soft (some dates are softer than others, so will need more cooking), then remove the pan from the heat and drain any liquid. Add the bicarbonate of soda.

Cream the butter and sugar together until light and fluffy, then add the eggs and beat well. Mix in the flour, date mixture and vanilla extract and pour into the prepared tin. Bake for 30–40 minutes, until just firm to the touch.

To make the sauce, boil the cream, sugar and treacle together. Pour over the top of the sponge until it is covered (there will be some left over), then place under a hot grill until it begins to bubble. Remove, cut into squares, and serve with the remaining sauce and a scoop of vanilla ice cream.

Trifle

Is there any dish less suited to its name than trifle? This glorious spectacle of a pudding is neither slight nor trivial. Or frivolous either. It requires hard work (baking the sponge, making the custard) and dedication. And it's miles removed from the school version, a sorry travesty and depressing mix of tinned fruit and lurid yellow custard (mixed from custard powder). Trifle has a long history, starting out as the bastard child of tipsy cake (sponge bathed in booze) and basic custard, little more than almond milk. Over time, the two dishes melded by way of a thickened, spiced cream to create this buxom queen of the festive table. It was a dish for the rich (good ones always were; the poor made do on scraps and gruel), but there's no authentic version. Aside from making everything fresh, a huge glass bowl is essential to show off all those lovely layers. If you are artistically inclined, the top of a trifle is a blank canvas on which to indulge your most outrageous candied fruit and petalled whims.

{ SERVES 6 }

For the sponge

50 g/1¾ oz butter, softened, plus extra to butter the dish
50 g/1¾ oz caster sugar
1 large egg, lightly beaten
50 g/1¾ oz self-raising flour, sifted

For the custard

600 ml/20 fl oz single cream
1 vanilla pod, split
3 eggs
4 egg yolks
50 g/1¾ oz caster sugar, plus extra for sprinkling
2 level teaspoons cornflour

For the layers

140 g/5 oz strawberry jelly tablet
4 tablespoons fino sherry
350 g/12 oz raspberries
300 ml/10 fl oz double cream
2 x 40 g/1½ oz Crunchie bars, roughly chopped
2 tablespoons flaked almonds, toasted

First, make the sponge. Preheat the oven to 180°C/350°F/Gas 4. Butter a 15 cm/6 inch round cake tin and line with baking parchment. Beat all the sponge ingredients together in a mixing bowl until smooth. Spoon into the tin, level the surface and bake for 20 minutes, or until lightly golden, well risen and the top springs back when lightly pressed with a fingertip. Leave to cool in the tin, then loosen the edges and turn out onto a wire rack to cool completely.

{ CONTINUES OVERLEAF }

To make the custard, put the cream into a saucepan with the vanilla pod and heat slowly, until it reaches boiling point. Leave to stand for 10–15 minutes for the flavours to develop. Remove the vanilla pod, scrape out the seeds and add to the cream. Discard the pod.

In a bowl, whisk the eggs, yolks, sugar and cornflour together until well mixed. Reheat the cream, then gradually whisk it into the egg mixture until smooth, using a balloon whisk. Return the mixture to the pan over a medium–low heat, stirring gently until thick. Put it into a bowl, whisk again, then sprinkle the surface with a little extra sugar or cover with a piece of crumpled and wetted non-stick baking parchment to prevent a skin from forming. Cover and transfer to the fridge to chill well.

Make up the jelly as directed on the packet, then allow it to cool. Slice the sponge and arrange it in the base of a 2.5 litre/4½ pint glass bowl. Douse in sherry until wet but not soggy. Top with a good layer of raspberries, keeping a few to decorate. Pour in the liquid jelly, cover and leave in the fridge to set.

Spoon the custard over the set jelly. Whisk the cream until it form soft swirls, then fold in two-thirds of the Crunchie. Spoon the cream over the custard and leave as soft waves. Sprinkle with the remaining Crunchie, raspberries and the flaked almonds. Chill until ready to serve.

Treacle tart

{ SERVES 4–6 }

225 g/8 oz shortcrust pastry
a little plain flour, for dusting
butter, for greasing
55 g/2 oz white bread, a couple of days old, crusts removed
225 g/8 oz golden syrup
juice of ½ small lemon
large pinch of ground ginger
1 small egg, beaten (optional)

A fine pudding, and one improved immeasurably by a hint of ginger and a squeeze of lemon juice. This was my favourite pudding when I was young, cooked by the brilliant Bridget, an immaculately coiffed cook with the most generous of bosoms. She made the finest treacle tart I ever tasted. This recipe is not my own, or even Bridget's, but is based on one taken from a classic pudding tome: the late Mary Norwak's *English Puddings, Sweet & Savoury* (Grub Street, 2004).

Preheat the oven to 180°C/350°F/Gas 4. Roll out the pastry on a lightly floured surface and use it to line a 20–23 cm/ 8–9 inch greased pie plate.

Tear the bread into small pieces and blitz in a food processor to make fine crumbs.

Gently warm the golden syrup and lemon juice in a saucepan, then stir in the breadcrumbs and ginger. Tip the mixture into the pastry case and spread evenly. Brush the edge of the pastry lightly and evenly with beaten egg if you wish. Bake for 20–25 minutes, until the pastry is golden. Serve hot or cold with cream.

Eccles cakes

{MAKES 12–14}

For the pastry
225 g/8 oz plain flour, sifted, plus extra for rolling out pastry
pinch of salt
175 g/6 oz cold unsalted butter, divided into 4 pieces
milk, to glaze

For the filling
115 g/4 oz currants
15 g/½ oz caster sugar, plus extra for glazing
large pinch of freshly grated nutmeg
40 g/1½ oz unsalted butter

The late Winnie Swarbrick was a magnificent lady and an incredible baker. Her ginger cakes, butter biscuits and chocolate cake, cooked in her small Goosnargh kitchen, are seared in my memory. And her Eccles cakes were the best in the world. She died last year, and is much missed.

To make the pastry, mix the flour and salt in a bowl, then rub a quarter of the butter into the flour. Add just enough water to form an elastic dough. Turn this out onto a lightly floured surface and use a rolling pin to roll it out into a rectangular strip about 15 x 35 cm/6 x 14 inches. Brush off any surplus flour.

Chop another quarter of the butter into cubes and dot it evenly over two-thirds of the pastry rectangle. Fold the pastry into three, bringing the end without fat to the centre, then folding over the other third. Press the pastry edges together with your fingers or a rolling pin, give the pastry a quarter turn so the folds are left and right, and roll out lightly. Cover and leave to rest in the fridge for an hour, then repeat the process of dotting with butter, folding and rolling twice more, resting the pastry for an hour each time.

While the pastry chills, make the filling. Mix the currants and caster sugar together, then add the nutmeg. While you are doing this, melt the butter. Pour the melted butter into the currant mixture and stir, then leave to cool. Preheat the oven to 180°C/350°F/Gas 4.

Roll out the pastry until it is 5 mm/¼ inch thick, then cut out 12 circles with a 7 cm/2¾ inch round cutter. Place a dessertspoon of the cooled currant mixture in the centre of each circle and draw the edges of pastry together. Turn the pastry over, smooth side up, and then roll lightly to flatten. Place on a lightly greased baking sheet.

Make 3 cuts in the top to show the filling, brush with milk and sprinkle with caster sugar. Bake for 15–20 minutes (check after 15 minutes), until golden.

Eccles cake ice cream

{ **MAKES ABOUT 800 ML/ 1½ PINTS** }

375 ml/13 fl oz full-fat milk
1 vanilla pod, split
100 g/3½ oz unrefined granulated sugar
4 egg yolks
250 ml/9 fl oz double cream
4 Eccles cakes (see recipe on page 80), torn to small shreds

I came up with this recipe when food writer Matthew Fort and I were invited to cook a dinner for that fine northern chef, Nigel Haworth, at Northcote Manor in Lancashire. I say 'cook', but we didn't do much of the hard graft, instead poncing about in chef's whites, marvelling at the professionalism and work of his 20-person brigade. Still, this recipe, combining classic French vanilla ice cream (based on a recipe in Caroline and Robin Weir's masterwork, *Ice Creams, Sorbets & Gelati – The Definitive Guide*, Grub Street, 2010) with these baked northern beauties, went down well. Even if the nearest thing I did to work was adding a sprig of something or other to the plate at the end. Some things are best left to the pros.

Combine the milk, vanilla pod and half the sugar in a saucepan and bring to the boil. Remove from the heat and set aside for 20 minutes. In a heatproof bowl, combine the egg yolks with the remaining sugar and beat with an electric whisk (or by hand, if you're feeling particularly energetic) until thick. Remove the vanilla pod from the milk, scrape out the seeds into the milk and discard the pod.

Bring the milk back to boiling point and then, whisking steadily, pour it in a slow, thin stream, into the yolks and sugar. Place the bowl over a pan of simmering water and stir with a spatula for about 15 minutes, until thick and smooth; the mixture should coat the back of the spatula. Cool the bowl by plunging the bottom into cold water, and leave the custard to cool.

Add the cream and stir. Put into an ice cream machine and churn for 25 minutes, or according to the manufacturer's instructions. Add the Eccles cake pieces 5 minutes before the end of the churning time. Serve straight from the machine or transfer to a plastic box and put in the freezer.

Rhubarb & ginger crumble

I'm not a pastry man. A maker of the stuff, I mean, rather than an eater, which I most certainly am. Too much precision needed, and patience, too. But crumble is different. Pinching sugar and flour into butter is always a soothing pleasure – just like the dish itself. It's actually a relatively modern invention, born from the strictures of rationing in World War II. Normal pastry used too much rare and precious flour, so someone came up with crumble. You don't want the topping too thick: no more than half an inch. It should flatter and add contrast to the soft filling, not overwhelm it.

Preheat the oven to 180°C/350°F/Gas 4. Melt the butter in a saucepan, add the rhubarb, sugar and grated ginger and cook until soft – about 5 minutes. Put into a shallow 1.2-litre/2-pint ovenproof dish.

To make the crumble, put the flour, butter and ground ginger into a bowl, and rub the butter into the flour until it resembles coarse breadcrumbs. Stir in half the sugar. Spread the crumble over the fruit and scatter with the remaining sugar. Bake for 45 minutes, or until the top is crisp and golden. Serve with cream or vanilla ice cream.

{ SERVES 4 }

15 g/½ oz unsalted butter
600 g/1 lb 5 oz rhubarb, cut into 5 cm/2 inch lengths
100 g/3½ oz light brown sugar
2 cm/¾ inch piece fresh root ginger, peeled and grated
double cream or vanilla ice cream, to serve

For the crumble topping
200 g/7 oz plain flour
100 g/3½ oz cold unsalted butter, diced
pinch of ground ginger
50 g/1¾ oz demerara sugar

Autumn pudding

{ SERVES 6 }

400 g/14 oz ripe plums
450 g/1 lb ripe blackberries
200 g/7 oz redcurrants
  or whitecurrants
100 g/3½ oz caster sugar
1 medium white loaf
double cream, to serve

This juice-stained beauty was originally known as 'hydropathic pudding', a rather clinical, dour name for such a splendid confection. But as it contained no pastry, it was seen as the sort of thing well suited to the diet of a spa. So after the enema, Scotch hose and Swiss shower, I'm pretty sure that this would come as sweet relief. I've changed the summer pudding to an autumn one, because I think all those blackberries, plums and redcurrants work even better than raspberries. The key is a balance of the sweet and tart. Use good bread, too. The cheap stuff, fine as it is for bacon sandwiches, tends to become slimy.

Wash the fruit and remove the stones, stalks and strings. Quarter the plums and put them in a saucepan with the sugar and 125 ml/4 fl oz water. Bring to the boil, then simmer gently for 5 minutes. Add the blackberries, cook for 3 minutes, then add the currants and cook for 3 minutes more, stirring from time to time until the fruit is tender but keeps its shape. Allow to cool slightly.

Line a 1.4 litre/2½ pint pudding basin with 2 long pieces of cling film so the base and sides are lined and the cling film drapes over the top edges of the basin. Cut the loaf into 1 cm thick slices then, using 8–9 slices depending on the size of the loaf, trim off the crusts. Cut a circle the size of the base of the basin, add to the basin, then cut 5–6 slices of bread in half and arrange around the sides of the basin, overlapping the edges slightly and pressing together.

Spoon in the warm fruit, reserving a little juice for serving, and cover with the remaining bread, again pressing the edges together. Fold the cling film over the top, cover with a small plate and weigh down with 2 cans of food. Put in the fridge overnight. Cover with a serving plate, invert the basin, then remove it. Peel off the cling film and brush any white patches with the reserved juice. Serve with lashings of cream.

Chocolate & orange soufflés

{ **SERVES 6** }

40g/1½oz butter, at
  room temperature
6 tablespoons caster sugar
3 large eggs, separated
4 level teaspoons cornflour
4 level teaspoons plain flour
2 level teaspoons cocoa
250 ml/9 fl oz milk
150 g/5½ oz dark chocolate,
  broken into pieces
grated rind of 1 medium orange
2 tablespoons orange juice
a little icing sugar, sifted,
  to decorate

Don't fear soufflés. They're very easy, despite what you might think. The key is to get air into your mixture, so it rises in the oven. And fold in the egg whites slowly, not fast as many recommend. Harold McGee, scientist and author of *On Food and Cooking* (1984), agrees, arguing that fast mixing will damage the foam. And what he says goes.

Preheat the oven to 190°C/375°F/Gas 5. Generously butter the inside of 6 x 150 ml/¼ pint ovenproof ramekin dishes right up to the top, reserving the remaining butter. Sprinkle 2 tablespoons sugar into the dishes, tilt to cover the insides of them with the sugar, then tip out the excess. Put the dishes on a baking sheet.

Whisk the egg yolks and remaining 4 tablespoons sugar in a bowl for a few minutes until thick and pale. Sift in the flours and cocoa, then mix briefly until smooth.

Pour the milk into a saucepan, bring to the boil, then gradually whisk into the egg mixture. Return to the pan and cook over a medium heat, stirring constantly, until thick and smooth. Take off the heat and add the chocolate and remaining butter, leave for a minute until melted, then stir in the orange rind and juice. Leave to cool for 10 minutes.

Whisk the egg whites in a large clean glass bowl until softly peaking. Fold a spoonful into the chocolate mixture to loosen it, then gently fold in the remaining whites. Divide among the dishes, run a finger around the edges, then bake for 12–15 minutes, until risen above the top of the dishes with a slight wobble in the centre. Dust with sifted icing sugar.

{ Quick fixes }

In a perfect world, we'd all cook every night, spending hours slaving over the stove to create dishes that would excite even the most leaden of palates. But after a long, dreary day at work, the last thing you usually want to do is slice a dozen carrots, brown meat and skim broth. You want to eat, and fast. I'd be a liar if I didn't admit to the odd (or not so odd) takeaway, as well as wrapping hastily torn chunks of cheese in pre-sliced white bread. Or eating ham by the fistful, straight from the packet. These are the quickest fixes of all, though they tend not to endear one to one's better half. The recipes in this section are a touch more civilised; they're all about ease and speed. Some may take longer than 30 minutes to marinate and cook, but none need more than 15 minutes (and that's 15 amateur minutes, not 15 of Marcus Wareing's or Jason Atherton's minutes) to prepare. And compared to the ghastly ready meal, these dishes will thrill and delight.

{ Steak }

There's no bore worse than a steak bore. Give them the chance, and they'll bang on for days, with all the spittle-specked, bright-eyed enthusiasm of a Jehovah's Witness going door-todoor. Eyes glaze over as they describe that hunk of 54-day-aged Belted Galloway they once ate in a steakhouse so exclusive that only the seventh son of a seventh son has a chance of being admitted through its hallowed doors. Or the sliver of sirloin chopped from a cow that was raised by virgins and that supped on the spring of eternal youth.

But really, the world is awash with average steak, the stuff that looks OK, tastes OK, but hardly lingers in the memory. Add a little butter, gravy or sauce and things improve. But truly great steak is a rare beast. Its creation is as much art as science.

Good breeding is not enough. Pure Angus, Longhorn and Devon Red are all wonderful native British breeds. But without the right feed (and grass is always best, with a little winter silage) or with amateur finishing (the process towards the end of a cow's life where the protein in feed is increased to create a good, hard layer of fat), you may as well be cutting into American feedlot pap. Then there's the age (older means more flavour), the slaughter (as stress-free as possible), the hanging and butchering. Muck up one stage and the whole thing's a busted flush.

Your choice of cut can help. None are better than the others, just different. Fillet is the most tender, as it has the least work to do when the animal is alive. Think of it as the dissolute but vacuous toff: fun every now and then, but can grate rather quickly. All that indolence makes for little depth. Sirloin is more middle-class in its work ethic, sitting above the fillet and taking part in light, white-collar labour. So it mixes pleasing texture with the prospect of taste. The rump is resolutely working class, a cut that has to toil for a living, shifting the hind legs and supporting the butt. The result – plenty of chew and, hopefully, character, too. These, of course, are outlines painted with the broadest of strokes. Good fillet can possess far more depth than run-of-the-mill rump. And humble skirt, sliced from a well-brought-up cow, will delight rather more than prime rib chopped from a bore.

As to cooking, unless you possess a professional grill that burns hotter than Hades, a heavy cast-iron griddle pan is best. Heat it over a high heat for at least 10 minutes. Then oil your steak (not the pan) and season with a heavy hand. For rare, I cook for 2 minutes each side and rest for 4. For medium, go for 3 minutes and rest for 6. For well done … well, as long as you want. The taste and texture would have left the building after 5 minutes each side anyway.

'Truly great steak is a rare beast. Its creation is as much art as science. Good breeding is not enough.'

Steak

{ SERVES 2 }

2 x 250–300 g/9–10 oz
   thick (about 5 cm/2 inch)
   sirloin steaks
groundnut or olive oil
sea salt and freshly ground
   black pepper

Let the steaks come to room temperature, covered. Heat a cast-iron griddle pan over a high heat for 10 minutes, until smoking.

Massage the steaks with oil and season with a heavy hand: lots of salt and generous with the pepper, too.

Place the steaks in the pan and *don't touch for 2 minutes*. No poking, prodding or general mucking about. Then turn them over and repeat. (For medium steaks, cook for 3 minutes each side.)

When time's up, remove to a warmed plate and rest for 4 minutes (6 minutes for medium). Serve with a crisp green salad.

Asian steak in lettuce

I once had to taste 30 steaks in a day. Being fundamentally greedy, I couldn't just take a slice of each. I started at a sprint, wolfing down great slabs of the first half-dozen. The pace did slow and, by the end, even thinking became vexed. I could barely move. Anyway, the next day saw my fridge filled with cold, cooked steak. So in a desperate bid to inject some greenery into my swollen, stolid gut, I sliced up the steak, covered it with herbs and cucumber, wrapped it in lettuce and dipped it in a fiery, lime-spiked fish sauce. Bliss, and it could even be described as healthy. Well, healthy*ish*, anyway.

Slice the steaks thinly across the grain and lay them on a plate. On separate plates, lay out the lettuce leaves, herbs and cucumber. Mix all the sauce ingredients together and put into a bowl.

To serve, take some steak, cup it in a lettuce leaf, cover in herbs and cucumber, wrap and dip in sauce. Repeat at will.

{ SERVES 4 AS A STARTER }

2 x 250–300 g/9–10 oz steaks, cooked (see left)
2 soft lettuces, leaves separated
handful of coriander, roughly chopped
handful of mint, roughly chopped
1 cucumber, cut into slivers

For the dipping sauce
6 tablespoons fresh lime
3 tablespoons fish sauce
5–10 bird's-eye chillies, chopped

Peas with pancetta

{ SERVES 4 }

4 tablespoons extra-virgin olive oil
100 g/3½ oz unsmoked pancetta, finely chopped
½ small onion, finely chopped
100 ml/3½ fl oz dry white wine (Verdicchio, if possible)
1.3 kg/3 lb fresh peas, shelled, or 400 g/14 oz shelled peas

Fresh peas have a sweetness that is impossible to match. But frozen peas are fine here, too. If you can't find pancetta, substitute bacon. This is a steadfast side dish.

Heat the oil in a large sauté pan over a medium heat and cook the pancetta until crisp and golden. Add the onion and sauté for 5 minutes, stirring frequently.

Add the wine, reduce the heat to medium-hot and simmer gently for a few minutes to reduce slightly. When the onion begins to soften, add the peas and cook for a further 2 minutes, stirring continuously. Serve immediately.

Spaghetti alla carbonara

{ SERVES 2 }

250 g/9 oz good smoked pancetta or smoked streaky bacon, diced
1 clove garlic, lightly bruised
350 g/12 oz spaghetti
sea salt and freshly ground black pepper
3 eggs, beaten
6 tablespoons freshly grated Parmesan

Forget all those horribly rich, cream-soaked aberrations they call carbonara. They usually have the texture of wallpaper paste, and sit uncomfortably in the belly for hours. This fairly proper version (and by this I mean better, not trainspotterly 'authentic') depends totally on the quality of the ingredients: good, fresh eggs, and proper smoked pancetta or decent smoked streaky bacon.

Fry the pancetta or bacon with the garlic over a medium heat until crisp. Remove the garlic. Drain the pancetta and set aside.

Cook the spaghetti in lots of boiling water, with a decent whack of salt, according to packet instructions. Drain.

Put the hot spaghetti into a clean warmed pan, throw over the eggs and mix well, then add pancetta/bacon and Parmesan, and season to taste with lots of black pepper. The egg mixture should cling to each strand but not become scrambled. Serve immediately.

Rack of lamb

This is an expensive cut, but nothing beats ripping just-pink chunks of lamb from the bone, then knawing off any last, juicy scraps. I could eat a whole rack myself, but then I'm a pig. One rack between two should do fine. As with all lamb, avoid the stuff that appears in early spring. It might seem traditional, but it ain't.

Preheat the oven to 220°C/425°F/Gas 7. Massage 1 tablespoon olive oil into the lamb, along with the herbs, salt and pepper, and leave for 10 minutes.

Heat the remaining oil in a heavy roasting pan over a high heat, then brown the rack all over: fat-side first for 3 minutes and bottom for 2. Put in the oven, fat-side up, and cook for 15 minutes. Rest for 5 minutes before serving with green salad and baked potatoes.

{ SERVES 2 }

1 x 6-bone rack of lamb, French-trimmed
2 tablespoons olive oil
handful of mixed rosemary and thyme, finely chopped
sea salt and freshly ground black pepper
green salad, to serve
baked potatoes, to serve

Griddled lamb with cucumber raita

{ SERVES 2 }

450 g/1 lb shoulder or leg of lamb, off the bone, fat removed
150 g/5½ oz natural yogurt
1 teaspoon ground coriander
pinch of ground cumin
pinch of freshly ground black pepper
juice of ½ lemon

For the cucumber and tomato raita
250 g/9 oz Greek yogurt
½ cucumber, deseeded and finely diced
4 tomatoes or 16 cherry tomatoes, finely chopped
2 tablespoons finely chopped coriander or mint
1 teaspoon ground cumin
sea salt and freshly ground black pepper

A fine summer dinner, this time with an Eastern Mediterranean scent. Despite reports to the contrary, the lamb we eat in spring is not much good. Tender, yes, but a total stranger to flavour. In the old days, spring was the time lambs were born, and they were eaten towards the end of summer, when they actually tasted of something. Even better, they were slaughtered at a year old, around hogget age. Nowadays, the market demands lamb for Easter, so we eat beasts that are born in October, and overwintered indoors, kept from those verdant shoots of sweet new grass. Hence the lack of lamby heft. Anything over a year, though, and you're looking at a tougher beast, better suited to braising than barbecuing or griddling.

Cut the lamb into 3 cm/1¼ inch chunks. Mix together the yogurt, coriander, cumin, black pepper and lemon juice in a bowl. Add the lamb, mix well, cover and leave to sit in the fridge for at least an hour.

To make the cucumber and tomato raita, mix the yogurt, cucumber, tomatoes, herbs and cumin together. Season to taste and chill, covered, until ready to serve. If barbecuing, get your coals good and hot.

When you are ready to cook the lamb, take it out of the marinade and season, but do not wipe off the marinade. Thread the meat onto metal skewers (or use wooden satay sticks that have been soaked in water for an hour to prevent them from catching fire).

Grill over a high heat for 8–10 minutes on the barbecue or griddle pan, turning and basting with the marinade every so often. Serve hot with the raita.

BBQ butterflied leg of lamb

{ SERVES 6 }

1.5 kg/3 lb 5 oz leg of lamb, butterflied (ask your butcher to do this)
2 cloves garlic, crushed
1 teaspoon hot paprika
2 tablespoons red wine vinegar
2 teaspoons thyme leaves, finely chopped
1 tablespoon olive oil
green salad, to serve
crusty rolls, to serve

This is a mighty fine barbecue dish, and very easy to make. Get your butcher to butterfly the leg of lamb. When cooking, ensure the flames don't roar out of control; this isn't a Burger King advert. You want grilled meat, not scorched flesh. Rest for at least 10 minutes, then carve into thick slices.

Put the lamb in a big bowl. Mix together the garlic, paprika, vinegar and thyme and rub into the lamb. Drizzle over the olive oil, cover and leave to marinate in the fridge overnight (or for a minimum of 2 hours), turning occasionally.

Take the lamb out of the fridge and allow to come up to room temperature and spark up the barbie. Wait until the flames have died down and the coals are covered with grey ash. Depending on the charcoal, this can take up to an hour.

Cook the lamb for about 10 minutes on each side (this gives a pink centre; for well done give it 15 minutes on each side), or until done to your liking. Leave to rest for 10 minutes before serving. Slice the lamb and serve with a green salad and crusty rolls.

A simple dish for bachelors & widowers to impress their guests

{ SERVES 2 }

1 onion, cut into wedges
3 cloves garlic, roughly chopped
sea salt and freshly ground black pepper
3 tablespoons dry white wine or dry sherry
3 tablespoons olive oil, plus extra for the chicken
2 chicken legs and 2 chicken thighs (the best you can afford)
juice of 1 lemon
green salad, to serve
baked potatoes, to serve

My father is a serious eater, but was never much of a cook. His only real speciality when we were children was steaks grilled on the top of the Aga in a toast rack. The result was near perfect, but did tend to leave an inch of smoking, blackened fat on the hob. My mother was always less than impressed. He later married Rose, who really knew her stuff. When she became ill, he took over the culinary reins and became, in the months before she died, a rather good cook. He's not one for faffing about with prissy presentation, and this dish takes under 5 minutes to prepare.

Preheat the oven to 180°C/350°F/Gas 4. Line a roasting tin with foil. Add the onion and garlic, season, then add the wine or sherry and olive oil.

Rub the chicken with a little more olive oil and add to the tin, skin-side down.

Cook for 45 minutes, or until cooked through, basting after 15 and 30 minutes. At 30 minutes, turn over the chicken legs. To check they're cooked, poke a skewer into the thickest part of the thigh: the juices should be golden, not pink. If not, cook for a little longer, then re-test.

Remove from the oven and allow to rest for 10 minutes. Sprinkle with a little more salt and the lemon juice. Serve with a green salad and baked potatoes.

Grilled Dover sole

{ SERVES 2 }

55 g/2 oz butter, melted
2 x 350 g/12 oz Dover sole, skinned and gutted, fins removed but head intact
sea salt and freshly ground black pepper
1 lemon, halved
buttered peas, to serve
sautéed waxy potatoes, to serve

For me, the sole is the greatest of all fish – with a price to match. That wonderful, near-gelatinous texture, the sweet, faintly uric flesh. Forget Escoffier and his 155 ways with this beautiful flat fish. You want it grilled, with butter and a good squeeze of lemon. This is a treat and demands to be served with peas and sautéed waxy potatoes.

Preheat the grill to maximum for about 15 minutes. Line the grill-pan with foil, brush with melted butter and put the fish on top. Paint the fish liberally with melted butter and season with salt and pepper, then cook for 4–6 minutes on one side. The tail should just start to smoulder.

Turn over and cook for another 2–3 minutes, until the flesh lifts easily off the bone. Serve with buttered peas and sautéed waxy potatoes.

Salt-baked sea bass

This is a grand, expensive and expansive dish, requiring a whole wild sea bass and a shedload of salt. Don't waste your Maldon on this one – use the cheapest sea salt you can buy. The salt solidifies in the heat and the fish arrives at the table entombed in a hard white mound. But inside its sodium chloride prison, the fish will have steamed in its own juices, untouched by the salt. A few cracks, a careful peel and you have the most splendidly succulent fish.

{ SERVES 4 }

1 kg/2 lb 4 oz sea salt
2 egg whites
4 slices of lemon
a few sprigs of dill (not too much, as it's quite a bully)
2 bay leaves
1 x 1 kg/2 lb 4 oz wild sea bass, scaled and gutted

Preheat the oven to 200°C/400°F/Gas 6. Line a roasting tin, a little larger than the fish, with foil. Mix the salt and egg whites together, then spread a thinnish layer about the shape and size of the fish, on the foil. Stuff the lemon, dill and bay into the fish cavity, then put the fish on the salt in the tin.

Mould the rest of the salt mixture over and around the fish to enclose it, patting it into place with your hands.

Bake for 25 minutes. Crack open with the handle of a big knife, peel away the salt and eat.

Spiced grilled mackerel

{ SERVES 4 }

4 mackerel, gutted
3 cloves garlic, crushed
1 tablespoon ground cumin
1 teaspoon ground coriander
½ teaspoon cayenne pepper
3 tablespoons olive oil
juice of ½ lemon
2 lemons, halved, to serve

Mackerel: the most underrated of fish. Cheap, sustainable and, when fresh, utterly divine. The problem is that after a few days it turns from hero to stinking zero. If you have a barbecue, use it. Everything tastes better when cooked over hot coals.

Slash each mackerel diagonally 3 or 4 times on each side, then place them in a bowl. Mix together the garlic, spices, olive oil and lemon juice, then rub the mixture all over the mackerel. Cover and put in the fridge to marinate for 20 minutes.

Heat a large griddle pan over a medium heat (or even better, heat a barbecue until hot, the flames have died down and the coals glow softly). Add the mackerel and cook for 3–5 minutes on each side, or until golden brown all over and cooked through (the flesh should be opaque and flake easily). Remove from the pan and serve with lemon to squeeze over the fish.

Kipper pâté

{ SERVES 4–6 }

4 x 300 g/10 oz good kippers
225 g/8 oz cream cheese
big pinch of hot paprika, or to taste
sea salt and freshly ground black pepper
2 tablespoons single cream
good toast, to serve
2 lemons, quartered, to serve

The only problem with grilling a kipper, anointed with a fat flake of butter, is that the fishy tang tends to linger. My late stepmother Rose used to implore my father to poach them instead. 'Not a chance,' he'd reply. 'Totally different taste.' A good kipper is a grand thing indeed, but for those of a more delicate constitution this classic kipper pâté is unbeatable.

Poach the kippers in simmering water for 3–4 minutes, then let them cool in the liquid. Remove the skin and bones and flake.

Using a plastic spatula – or ideally a food processor – work the cream cheese into a smooth cream, adding paprika, salt and black pepper to taste. Stir in the cream and then gradually work the kipper into the mixture. When smooth, chill, covered, for an hour. Serve with good toast and a few quarters of lemon.

Clam fritters

Gloriously easy to make, and equally good as a snack or light supper. Or even a canapé, if you're that way inclined.

Put the clams and wine in a saucepan over a medium heat, cover tightly and steam over a high heat for 2–3 minutes, or until the clams have opened. Discard any that fail to open.

Lift out the clams and, using a slotted spoon, take out the meat and chop finely.

Strain the remaining wine and clam juice into a clean pan and boil for 3–4 minutes to reduce by half. Taste. If too salty, leave out the salt from the batter.

To make the batter, sift the flour and salt together. Beat in the egg and add the reduced wine/clam broth. Mix until it has the consistency of porridge, then mix in the clam meat, cayenne and chopped parsley.

Pour oil into a medium saucepan until about one-third full and heat until a little batter dropped into it bubbles immediately. Drop the fritter mixture, a teaspoon at a time, into the hot oil. Remove with a slotted spoon when nut-brown. Drain on kitchen paper and serve immediately.

{ MAKES ABOUT 20 }

about 50 clams, rinsed and scrubbed if necessary, discarding any open or broken shells
200 ml/7 fl oz dry white wine
70 g/2½ oz plain flour
½ teaspoon salt
1 egg, beaten
½ teaspoon cayenne pepper
handful of parsley, finely chopped
sunflower oil, for deep frying

Marinated prawns

{ SERVES 2 }

12 very fresh raw prawns
juice of 1 lemon
2 tablespoons extra-virgin olive oil
sea salt and freshly ground black pepper
handful of flat-leaf parsley, finely chopped

This dish is totally dependent on the quality and freshness of the prawns. Best of all are those Italian beauties, the *gambero rosso*, with scarlet body and the sweetest of flesh. You can use any type of prawn, as long they are uncooked, not previously frozen and ideally just hauled from the sea. If the antennae are still on, it's a good sign, as they drop off within hours of capture.

Clean the prawns: gently pull off the heads and shells, but leave the tails on and then use a toothpick to remove the black, thread-like gut.

In a small bowl, whisk together the lemon juice and olive oil to emulsify; season well, then stir in the parsley.

Dip the prawns in the marinade, then put them on a plate, cover and refrigerate for 30 minutes.

Remove from the fridge, re-dip the prawns in the marinade and serve.

Hot buttered crab

This is best made with a freshly picked crab, using both brown and white meat.

Preheat the grill to hot. Put the crabmeat into a bowl and mix with the nutmeg, olive oil, sherry vinegar, a big dash of Tabasco and the salt and pepper. Add about three-quarters of the breadcrumbs and all the butter. Mix well.

Spoon the mixture into the cleaned crab shells (or into 2 shallow ovenproof dishes), cover with the remaining breadcrumbs, then place under the grill for 5 minutes, or until golden and piping hot.

{ SERVES 2 }

2 x 1 kg/2 lb 4 oz boiled crabs, picked – yielding about 400 g/14 oz white meat and 250 g/9 oz dark meat – and shells cleaned
a very fine grating of nutmeg
1 tablespoon olive oil
2 tablespoons sherry vinegar
Tabasco
sea salt and freshly ground black pepper
75 g/3 oz fresh breadcrumbs
50 g/1¾ oz butter, melted

Proper crab cakes

{ SERVES 2 }

225 g/8 oz cooked white crabmeat
115 g/4 oz cooked brown crabmeat
2 teaspoons plain flour
1 egg yolk
½ teaspoon Tabasco
¼ teaspoon Worcestershire sauce
pinch of sea salt
large pinch of cayenne pepper
85 g/3 oz fine breadcrumbs
2–3 tablespoons olive oil
1–2 lemons, cut into wedges, to serve

I'm fed up with those recipes that demand more potato than crab. Here, you actually get to taste the fat hunks of brown and white meat. Both are essential. You can pick your own meat (it's easy, if time-consuming) or buy it fresh from the fishmonger. Don't bother with the pasteurised stuff for this recipe – the sweetness has long departed.

Mix the crabmeat with the flour, then mix in the egg yolk, Tabasco, Worcestershire sauce, salt and cayenne.

Put the breadcrumbs in a shallow dish. Shape some of the crab mixture into a plum-sized cake, then roll in the breadcrumbs, patting gently to cover. Repeat until you have used all the crab mixture.

Heat the olive oil in a frying pan until very hot, then cook the crab cakes for about 3 minutes on each side, until golden brown. They're fragile and crumbly, so turn carefully. Drain on kitchen paper and serve with wedges of lemon.

Griddled asparagus with duck egg

As with any asparagus dish, this is only worth doing with English asparagus, in season from the end of April to the start of June. The natural sugars turn to starch within moments of being cut. Get them as fresh as you can, with pert stalks, tight tips and a base that isn't too woody. Try to buy direct from the source. Even better, pick your own. I once heard of a man so obsessed with eating asparagus fresh that he camped out beside his crown of asparagus the night before he was due to harvest them. As the sun rose the next day, the water was already boiling on a propane stove. At first light, he cut a dozen, simmered them quickly and ate with a pinch of salt. His verdict: pretty damned good. For the rest of us, a few hours journey from field to fork is fine. The duck eggs ooze their wonderful richness over the green stalks: the perfect partner to this late-spring feast.

{ SERVES 2 }

12 asparagus spears
extra-virgin olive oil
sea salt and freshly ground
  black pepper
2 duck eggs
2 slices of good bread

Heat a griddle pan over a high heat. Brush the asparagus spears with olive oil and season with salt and pepper. Cook on the griddle for 3–4 minutes, until the stems are tender to the tip of a sharp knife. Keep warm.

To poach the duck eggs, use a frying pan with a lid: half-fill with water, bring to the boil, crack in the eggs, cover the pan, remove from the heat and leave for 3 minutes. Drain on kitchen paper.

Toast the bread on the griddle pan until it is crisp, with good charred markings. Top each slice of toast with the griddled asparagus and perch a poached duck egg on top.

Jeremy's baked asparagus

{ SERVES 4–5 }

sea salt and freshly ground black pepper
20 asparagus spears, woody stems trimmed
1 x 120 g packet (10 sheets) *feuilles de brick*
100 g/3½ oz unsalted butter, melted and kept just warm
40 g/1½ oz Parmesan, finely grated
a little olive oil, for greasing

Jeremy Lee is not only one of our finest cooks ('Cook, darling, not chef') but also one of the kindest, funniest and most intelligent men you'll ever meet. He's now cooking at Quo Vadis in London, and his food is sublime. Of course, this dish only dances onto his menu during spring, made with the freshest British asparagus. But eaten with the fingers, and washed down with blood orange and Campari, it puts a real, *um*, spring into one's step.

If the asparagus is tough-skinned, the pleasure in eating is diminished. Peeling the stalk will set this to rights. *Feuilles de brick* is a Tunisian pastry similar to filo, but cut into large circles.

Preheat the oven to 200°C/400°F/Gas 6. Bring a large pot of salted water to the boil and plunge in the asparagus spears. Pop on a lid and bring the water back to the boil. Remove the lid and boil furiously until the asparagus is tender.

Lift the asparagus from the pot, plunge it into iced water, then drain on kitchen paper before laying it on a tray to cool.

Lay one sheet of pastry on a clean surface, covering the remaining pastry with a damp tea-towel to prevent it from drying out. Brush lightly with butter, sprinkle on some of the Parmesan and season lightly with salt and pepper. Cut the sheet in half and lay a spear of asparagus along the cut edge of each half. Roll the spears tightly in the pastry: you end up with curious-looking sticks, like very long cigarettes. Lay these on a lightly oiled baking sheet and repeat until all the asparagus is wrapped. Put in the fridge for 10 minutes or so to rest.

Put the baking sheets, one or two at a time, in the hot oven and bake for 7–8 minutes, until the pastry is golden brown. Heap on a plate, sprinkle Parmesan all over and serve swiftly.

Porcini with pappardelle

The porcini, cep, or penny bun is not exactly the best-looking of wild mushrooms. With its stout stalk and shiny pate, it's the Mr Pickwick of the forest floor. It's another particularly generous Antonio Carluccio feast.

Heat the oil and half the butter in a large frying pan until medium hot. Add the mushrooms, salt and pepper, and increase the heat once the liquid starts to bubble.

Meanwhile, cook the pasta in a large saucepan of salted boiling water. If using fresh, it'll take no more than a couple of minutes. If dried, cook according to the packet instructions. Drain.

Add the garlic to the frying pan and cook for a few more minutes, stirring, until the mushrooms take on a tan. Throw in the parsley, then stir into the cooked pasta and serve immediately. Toss with the remaining butter and a drizzle of extra-virgin olive oil.

{ SERVES 4 }

2 tablespoons olive oil, plus extra to serve
40 g/1½ oz butter
500 g/1 lb 2 oz fresh porcini, sliced vertically (you can use chanterelles or field mushrooms)
sea salt and freshly ground black pepper
500 g/1 lb 2 oz pappardelle (fresh is best, but dried will do)
2 cloves garlic, finely chopped
handful of flat-leaf parsley, finely chopped

Purple-sprouting broccoli with chillies & anchovies

{ SERVES 2 OR 4 AS A SIDE DISH }

500 g/1 lb 2 oz purple-sprouting broccoli (or regular broccoli, cut into small florets)
2 tablespoons olive oil
2 cloves garlic, finely sliced
1 hottish red chilli (long, thin one or jalapeño), finely sliced
6 anchovy fillets (those packed in salt are best, but there are some decent ones packed in oil too), roughly chopped

Preserved anchovies … the secret Samaritan. A bit like the Beast or the Hunchback of Notre Dame. Ugly, feared and misunderstood. But possessing a true heart of gold.

Definitely an acquired taste when eaten raw, once cooked they somehow melt into the background, providing a savoury backbone to any dish. Fish sauce, made from fermented fish, and central to most Southeast Asian cookery, performs a similar role.

Purple-sprouting broccoli is a seasonal treat and one of the few things to emerge from the garden in the lean months of March and April. You can use normal broccoli instead, and that 'tender-stem' stuff they sell in the supermarket works beautifully here, too.

Steam the broccoli for 5 minutes.

Heat the oil in a wok or large saucepan over a low heat, and cook the garlic and chilli very gently for about 5 minutes, making sure they don't burn. Add the anchovies, remove from the heat and bash with a wooden spoon until you have a fine-ish mulch.

Return the pan to the heat, add the broccoli and cook gently for a further 5–7 minutes. Serve hot.

Buttered leeks

{ SERVES 4–6 }

10 leeks, roughly chopped into rounds – discard only the white root ends and very extremities of green
250 g/9 oz good salted butter, chopped
freshly ground black pepper

Another of the dishes of my youth, this is as easy to make as it is calorific. Despite a hatred of all those anti-fat finger-waggers, this certainly verges on the, well, indulgent. You could put a pat of butter onto a Dan Brown book and it would taste good. But this is a fine winter dish, and goes wonderfully with most things.

Preheat the oven to 170°C/325°F/Gas 3.

Wash the leeks and allow to dry. Place them in a large ovenproof dish. Distribute the butter evenly over them, season with pepper, then bake for 25 minutes until the leeks are just tender.

{ Salads }

'I cheerfully forget my debtors, but I'll never pardon iceberg lettuce'. So wrote the late Ogden Nash, in *Ogden Nash Food* (Stewart, Tabori, and Chang, 1989). And while my sensibilities are not quite as affronted by the iceberg lettuce, he does have a point. I love those soft, floppy lettuces, pulled fresh from the garden. They might be less model-like than the iceberg, with its fixed grin and crisp edges. But the flavour is so much better.

A perfect green salad is high art indeed. The dressing must have just the right amount of acidity to cut through the green, but not so much that it puckers the tongue. Each leaf must be washed, then properly dried (buy a salad spinner) so that the dressing sticks. And the amount of dressing is key. Enough to caress, rather than smother the leaves. Four parts good oil to one of vinegar. And a decent whack of either smooth Dijon or English mustard. As to the vinegar, white wine is a good all-purpose choice, while sherry, red and rice have their own charms.

But there's far more to the salad than mere leaves. Chicken, chorizo, beans, chillies, fennel and orange are all key players. These aren't salads to pick at, but to proper food, for serious eaters.

Chicken liver & chorizo salad

{ SERVES 2 }

1 tablespoon plain flour
salt and freshly ground
  black pepper
6 chicken livers, about
  250 g/9 oz, cleaned and diced
1 tablespoon olive oil
1 small spicy chorizo sausage,
  about 100 g/3½ oz, cut into
  5 mm/¼ inch thick slices
2 tablespoons fino sherry
mixed salad leaves, such as baby
  gem lettuce and watercress
250 g/9 oz cherry
  tomatoes, halved
crusty bread, to serve

For the dressing

4 tablespoons extra-virgin
  olive oil
1 tablespoon red wine vinegar,
  or to taste

This is a salad with real punch, contrasting crisp coins of chorizo with tender chunks of chicken liver. Any excess richness is cut through by the sherry and vinegar. A true Iberian feast.

Season the flour with salt and pepper. Coat the chicken livers in the flour, shaking off any excess. Cover and set aside.

Heat the olive oil in a heavy-based frying pan over a medium–high heat and fry the chorizo for 3–4 minutes, or until crisp. Use a slotted spoon to remove it onto a warm plate, leaving the chorizo-flavoured oil in the pan.

Add the chicken livers to the pan and fry for 2–3 minutes, or until golden brown and just cooked through. Do not overcook. Remove the livers from the pan and add to the chorizo.

Pour off any excess oil from the pan, leaving behind the juices. Return the pan to the heat, pour in the sherry and stir to deglaze, scraping up any flavoursome brown bits from the bottom of the pan.

To make the dressing, in a small bowl whisk together the olive oil and vinegar with a pinch of salt and freshly ground black pepper. Taste and add more olive oil or vinegar if necessary. Put the mixed leaves and tomatoes in a bowl and pour enough dressing over to coat lightly; toss gently.

Divide the salad between 2 serving plates, then scatter over the chorizo and chicken livers, pour over the pan juices and serve with crusty bread.

Cos & haddock salad

This might seem an incongruous combination on paper but it works beautifully on the plate. The fennel not only adds flavour, but extra texture in contrast to the soft fish and cos lettuce.

Halve the fennel lengthwise. Cut out the small triangular core, trim the ends and discard. Slice the remaining fennel as thinly as possible.

Trim the lettuce hearts. Halve lengthways, halve again and cut each quarter into half. Rinse and shake dry.

To make the dressing, in a large bowl, whisk together the vinegar, lemon juice, mustard and olive oil. Season with salt, pepper and a pinch of sugar.

Toss the fennel and cos in the dressing to coat. Season the flour with salt and pepper and dust the fish fillets. Heat the olive oil in a frying pan over a medium–high heat and, when hot, lay in the fillets. Cook for 2–3 minutes on each side, or until the fish is light golden and cooked through.

Divide the salad between 2 plates, top with the fish and sprinkle with chives.

{ SERVES 2 }

1 small fennel bulb
3 hearts of cos or
  romaine lettuce
2 tablespoons plain flour
salt and freshly ground
  black pepper
2 x 175 g/6 oz haddock fillets
1 tablespoon olive oil
1 tablespoon chopped chives,
  to serve

For the dressing

½ tablespoon white wine vinegar
squeeze of lemon juice
1 teaspoon smooth
  Dijon mustard
1 tablespoon extra-virgin
  olive oil
pinch of caster sugar

Smoked eel & bacon salad

{ SERVES 2 }

8 rashers smoked bacon
400 g/14 oz smoked eel fillet, broken into big chunks
1 head of curly endive, separated, washed and dried in a salad spinner

For the dressing
juice of ½ lemon
½ teaspoon English mustard
1 teaspoon fresh horseradish or ½ teaspoon commercial
salt and freshly ground black pepper
3 tablespoons extra-virgin olive oil

I love eel. Far from the sinister, flesh-eating beasts of popular imagination, they're actually remarkable creatures, whose life cycle makes the salmon look laid-back. Born somewhere in the vast, strange mass that is the Sargasso Sea, they float over thousands of miles as *leptocephali* – gossamer, leaf-like larvae – at the mercy of predators both above and below, before turning into tiny elvers when they hit brackish water. It's then upstream to find a home and hang about for a few years before fattening up for the journey back home. Epic, in every way.

The British eel fisheries are very well run, but worldwide, stocks are plummeting. Try to buy British and you can eat with conscience clear. The best smoked eel I've ever eaten is from Brown and Forrest in Somerset. Quite incredible. Severn & Wye do a fine product too. If salad seems too insubstantial, pile it into a good baguette with extra mayonnaise and eat as a sandwich.

To make the dressing, mix the lemon juice with the mustard, horseradish, salt and pepper. Whisk in the oil to emulsify.

Cook the bacon in a frying pan over a high heat until crisp. Crumble it into biggist pieces.

Mix the eel and bacon with the endive in a serving bowl, pour the dressing over and serve.

Green salad

{ SERVES 2 }

3 hearts of cos lettuce or 1 floppy lettuce, leaves separated, washed and dried

For the dressing
1 tablespoon white wine vinegar
½ teaspoon smooth French or English mustard
sea salt and freshly ground black pepper
4 tablespoons good extra-virgin olive oil

Put the lettuce in a bowl. To make the dressing, mix the vinegar with the mustard, then add a big pinch of salt and a healthy grind of pepper. Whisk in the oil, slowly, so it's properly mixed, or just add and shake in a jam jar.

Carefully dress the salad, a few dribbles at a time, until each leaf is gleaming, not drowning. Finish with a small pinch of salt.

Provençal green bean salad

This reminds me of long, rosé-fuelled lunches at a friend's house in the south of France. You want to cook the beans to just past the squeak point, but not so they're soft and dreary. Use the best olive oil you can find. And do top and tail the beans. Chef Simon Hopkinson is very particular about this and once sent back a plateful of these *haricots verts* because only the tops were trimmed. He wasn't being fussy, just aesthetically exacting.

Cook the beans in well-salted boiling water for 6 minutes. Drain and refresh in cold water.

Soften the garlic in 1 tablespoon olive oil over a low heat for about 3–4 minutes, then add to the beans along with the remaining olive oil, the vinegar and salt and pepper to taste.

{ SERVES 4 }

1 kg/2 lb 4 oz green beans topped and tailed
sea salt and freshly ground black pepper
2 cloves garlic, very finely chopped
2–3 tablespoons extra-virgin olive oil
2 teaspoons white wine vinegar

Oriental cucumber salad

This is one of those dishes that started off rather different to what it is now. I love the crisp, cool flavour of cucumber salad and, mixed with the chicken, chillies, rice wine vinegar and fish sauce, it suddenly becomes an incredibly healthy dinner. Marinating the meat in *gochujang* (Korean fermented chilli paste), available from Thai supermarkets, adds another layer of flavour. And the two different cuts of the cucumber add an interesting texture. Cool cucumber and hot chicken. Nice.

Put the chicken in a glass bowl and mix with 1 tablespoon of the fish sauce, the juice of 1 lime and the *gochujang*. Cover and leave to marinate in the fridge for a few hours.

Put all the cucumber in another bowl with 1 tablespoon of fish sauce, the juice of ½ lime, the rice wine vinegar and all the chillies. Mix well and check the taste: you may like to add more fish sauce. Cover and set aside in the fridge for 2 hours.

Add the broccoli, spring onions and shallots to the cucumber, re-cover and marinate in the fridge for a further 30 minutes.

Tip the marinated cucumber mixture into a sieve set over a bowl, reserving any liquid.

Heat the oil in a wok or frying pan over a high heat until smoking. Fry the chicken for 12–15 minutes, turning from time to time, until cooked through and a little crisp at the edges.

In a large bowl, mix the marinated cucumber mixture with the chopped herbs and cooked chicken. Add some of the reserved cucumber marinade, along with the juice of ½ a lime. Taste and check there's enough fish sauce (there should be a balance of hot, salty and a little sour) and serve.

{ SERVES 2 }

2 chicken breasts (the best you can afford), cut into 2 cm/¾ inch cubes
2 tablespoons fish sauce
juice of 2 limes
1 tablespoon *gochujang* (Korean fermented chilli paste) – or if you can't get this, use 1 tablespoon good Caribbean thick hot sauce
4 cucumbers, 3 shaved into ribbons using a potato peeler, 1 cut into 7.5 cm/3 inch long batons
2 tablespoons Japanese rice wine vinegar
4–8 bird's-eye chillies, or 1 Scotch bonnet, roughly chopped
½ head of broccoli, cut into thin slices
5 spring onions, sliced diagonally, about 1 cm/ ½ inch long
6 shallots (Thai if possible), roughly chopped
1 tablespoon groundnut oil
handful of mint, roughly chopped
big handful of coriander, roughly chopped

Fennel & orange salad

{ SERVES 2 }

2 largish fennel bulbs
3 oranges
handful of fresh broad beans
  (optional)

For the dressing
juice of ½ orange
juice of ½ lemon
sea salt and freshly ground
  black pepper
3–4 tablespoons extra-virgin
  olive oil

This is a reveille of a salad: fresh and punchy. Fennel and orange make perfect partners. And if you're making this in early summer, a handful of fresh broad beans makes things better still.

Cut the horns off the fennel bulbs, then use a mandolin to slice the bulbs from top to bottom.

Slice off both ends of the oranges, then remove all the peel and pith using a small sharp knife. Carefully cut out the segments.

If using broad beans, dunk them in boiling water, then immediately drain and rinse in cold water and peel.

To make the dressing, mix the orange and lemon juice, season, then whisk in the olive oil (you need twice as much oil as juice).

Divide the fennel, oranges and broad beans, if using, between 2 serving plates. Pour the dressing over and serve.

Orange, red onion & basil salad

{ SERVES 2 }

2 good oranges
1 red onion, sliced into thin rings
10 cherry tomatoes, halved
handful of basil, torn

For the dressing
big squeeze of lemon juice
2 tablespoons extra-virgin olive oil
sea salt and freshly ground black pepper

One of the most refreshing salads I've ever eaten: the orange works in deft harmony with the onion, cutting a wonderfully zingy path through the palate.

Slice off both ends of the oranges. Remove all the peel and pith using a small sharp knife, then cut into horizontal slices. Arrange the orange slices on a plate – nothing too anal, just keep it neatish. Scatter over the onion and tomatoes.

In a small bowl, whisk together the lemon juice and olive oil to emulsify; season well, then drizzle over the onions and tomatoes. Scatter with the basil.

{ Savouries }

Those with a keen interest in affairs of the gut need no introduction to the savoury, that crowning glory of Victorian and Edwardian eating. It arrived in the gap between pudding and fruit. And in the words of Ambrose Heath, who devoted an entire tome, *Good Savouries* (1934), to the matter, they make '… an admirable ending to a meal, like some unexpected witticism or amusing epigram at the close of a pleasant conversation. It has the last word, as it were, before we turn to the frivolities of dessert.'

Of course, the French were appalled by the very concept. 'A savoury, or rather a savoury dish coming at the very end of a dinner,' wrote P Morton Shand in *A Book of Food* (1927), 'is regarded by the French as something worse than an anachronism, a deliberate blasphemy against Gastronomea, Brillat-Savarin's Tenth Muse.' No matter, he goes on, for '… the course is an essentially English institution. The French loss is our gain.' Quite right too.

These bite-sized morsels were usually strong flavoured and toast-based (with the occasional pastry case or soufflé), all possessing those qualities so admired by Mrs Beeton, the 'piquant, rather strong, appetising flavour essential in a savoury.' Cheese played a starring role, along with anchovies, cured pork and all manner of devilled delights. Welsh rabbit and angels on horseback, soft roes on toast and curried croutes. As a man whose tastes tend towards the savoury, they represent a release from the tyranny of pudding. If you can't face adding in this extra exquisite course, the following make fine snacks and starters, too.

'Robustly and triumphantly English'

P Morton Shand, A Book of Food (Jonathan Cape, 1927)

Devilled kidneys on toast

{ SERVES 2 }

6 lamb's kidneys, about 350 g/12 oz total weight
3 tablespoons plain flour
1 teaspoon cayenne pepper
1 teaspoon mustard powder
sea salt and freshly ground black pepper
2 teaspoons butter
6 tablespoons chicken stock
few drops of Tabasco
1 teaspoon Worcestershire sauce
2 pieces of white toast

In Victorian and Edwardian times, the British were great fans of devilled everything. A pinch of cayenne pepper, some mustard, a splash of anchovy or Worcestershire sauce and a good knob of butter do wonders to any dish: almonds, biscuits, cutlets and sardines. Florence White, in *Good Things in England* (1932), mentions a recipe for Boodle's Club Devilled Bones. And very fine they sounded, too. To me the greatest savory of all is devilled kidneys. This is a proper breakfast dish, but equally civilised for lunch, tea or dinner. You can use lamb or veal kidneys, but make sure they're fresh, and core them yourself with a pair of scissors.

Snip the white cores out of the kidneys using scissors, rinse with cold water, drain and pat dry with kitchen paper.

Mix the flour, cayenne, mustard powder and salt and pepper together on a plate. Dust the kidneys with the seasoned flour and shake to remove excess.

Heat a frying pan over a medium–high heat, add the butter and fry the kidneys for 2 minutes each side, or until cooked. Add the stock, Tabasco and Worcestershire sauce, to taste.

Remove the kidneys from the pan and keep warm. Simmer the sauce for a minute or two until reduced slightly. Serve the kidneys on toast and pour the sauce over.

Crab toasts

You can use pasteurised vacuum-packed crab here, as flavours are bold.

Preheat the grill to hot. Mix the white and brown crabmeat with the butter, vinegar, lemon juice, mustard, Worcestershire sauce and Tabasco. Season with salt and cayenne pepper, taste and adjust as necessary.

Spread the mixture on toast, sprinkle with the grated cheese then grill for 2 minutes. Sprinkle with the parsley and serve.

{ SERVES 4 }

1 x 1 kg/2 lb 2 oz boiled crab, picked (or use pasteurised crab, about 200 g/7 oz white meat and 115 g/4 oz dark meat)
1 tablespoon butter, melted then cooled
1 tablespoon white wine vinegar
juice of ¼ lemon
1 teaspoon English mustard
½ teaspoon Worcestershire sauce
few drops of Tabasco
pinch of sea salt
pinch of cayenne pepper
4 pieces of brown toast
50 g/1¾ oz good strong Cheddar, grated
pinch of finely chopped parsley

English rabbit

{ SERVES 2 }

4 tablespoons decent English ale
150 g/5½ oz strong Cheddar, grated
1 teaspoon Worcestershire sauce
2 teaspoons freshly made English mustard
freshly ground black pepper
3 thick slices of good bread

The classic savoury, and basically cheese on toast with a few quid in its back pocket, this is an Anglicised version of Welsh rabbit. Ale, Worcestershire sauce, Cheddar and English mustard – fine, upstanding ingredients all, stalwarts of the Albion kitchen.

No one can agree as to whether this is 'rabbit' or 'rarebit'. The latter means a delicacy, and could have been corrupted into 'rabbit.' But 'rabbit' appeared in print before rarebit, in Hannah Glasse's *The Art of Cookery Made Plain and Easy* (1747) for a start. Who knows? It tastes equally good, whichever way it's spelt.

For the ale, an IPA works well but you don't want anything too heavy, as it tends to overwhelm and bludgeon the cheese into submission. Montgomery's Cheddar is the best in the world (along with Keen's), but if you can't find it, then substitute another strong, decent Cheddar.

Preheat the grill to hot. Put the ale in a saucepan and bring to the boil to burn off the alcohol and reduce slightly. Take the pan off the heat and stir in the cheese, until melted. Add the Worcestershire sauce, mustard and pepper.

Preheat the grill to hot. Toast one side of the bread under the grill, turn over, make an indentation and pour in the cheese. Grill for a minute or two and eat standing up. This is a dish that rarely makes it to the table.

Mushrooms on toast

This is quick fix comfort food of the finest variety, season of mellow fruitfulness on a plate. Wild mushrooms are best, anything from porcini and chanterelles – all sexy and yellow – to shaggy inkcaps, hedgehog and horse, parasol and fairy ring. They're free and, if you know where to look, abundant. When setting off on the 'silent hunt', ensure you know what you're looking for. *A Passion for Mushrooms* by Antonio Carluccio is comprehensive, as are Roger Phillips's *Wild Food* and Richard Mabey's *Food for Free*. If I'm not sure, I check about four tomes until certain. Death Caps and Destroying Angels live up to their name. And severe liver poisoning, or agonising death, can prove a real downer on dinner.

Heat the oil and butter in a frying pan over a medium heat until foaming. Add the mushrooms and stir, for about 2 minutes, until the juices start to bubble.

Throw in the garlic, lemon juice, salt and pepper and cook for another few minutes, until the mushrooms begin to take on colour. When soft, brown and a little shrunken, throw in the parsley and mix.

Anoint the bread with olive oil and cook on a griddle pan over a high heat until crisp and golden. Pile the mushrooms on top of the toast. The juices should soak through.

{ SERVES 2 }

1 tablespoon olive oil, plus extra for the bread
25 g/1 oz butter
300 g/10 oz wild mushrooms, such as porcini and chanterelles (or even button mushrooms, when wild are out of season)
2 cloves garlic, chopped
squeeze of lemon juice
sea salt and freshly ground black pepper
handful of flat-leaf parsley, roughly chopped
2 big slices of good bread

Rhubarb fool

{ SERVES 6 }

1.5 kg/3 lb 5 oz rhubarb, cut into 4 cm/1½ inch lengths
300 g/10½ oz caster sugar
juice and grated zest of 1 orange
568 ml/1 pint double cream
200 g/7 oz ginger biscuits, crushed
about 125 ml/4 fl oz King's Ginger liqueur or Stone's Ginger wine (optional)

Great name, and beautifully simple to make. Rhubarb is my favourite version. Ginger biscuits add wonderful crunch. Soaking them in King's Ginger liqueur makes it finer still. As summer goes on, use gooseberries or raspberries instead.

Preheat the oven to 180°C/350°F/Gas 4. Put the rhubarb in a casserole and sprinkle with the sugar, orange juice and zest. Cover with a lid and roast for about 40 minutes, until soft. Allow to cool. Strain the juice and reserve; pick out 18 pieces of rhubarb for decoration and set aside. Purée the remaining rhubarb in a food processor.

Whip the cream until it forms soft peaks, not too firm, then fold in the rhubarb purée along with a few dribbles of the reserved juice. Don't mix too manically.

Put a layer of crushed biscuits into 6 wine glasses, then a splash of the ginger booze. Spoon the fool on top and finish with 3 pieces of rhubarb.

Lemon granita

{ SERVES 4–6 }

500 ml/18 fl oz water,
  filtered if possible
200 g/7 oz caster sugar
250 ml/9 fl oz fresh lemon juice
  (you will need about 6 lemons)
vodka (optional)

You'll find granita all over southern Italy and Sicily, served in bars and sold from the side of the road. The ones made with lemons from Sorrento are particularly good. The key is the balance between sharp and sweet. And although this recipe seems a little hard going (well, not that hard), it is the best way to ensure you get those perfectly sized pieces of chipped ice. The technique comes from the wonderful *Ice Creams, Sorbets & Gelati –The Definitive Guide* (Grub Street, 2010) by Caroline and Robin Weir. They've forgotten more about their subject than I can ever hope to learn.

Bring 200 ml/7 fl oz of the water to the boil. Put the sugar in a bowl and pour over the boiling water. Stir until the sugar dissolves, then allow to cool. Add the lemon juice and remaining water to the sugar syrup, stir and chill in the fridge for at least 3 hours.

Pour into a strong plastic container, about 25 x 25 x 8 cm/19 x 10 x 3 inches: the mixture should be about 2 cm/¾ inch deep. Freeze for 1 hour, until the edges start to ice and the bottom starts to freeze. Beat hard with fork, scraping every frozen bit away from the sides and bottom and remixing with the liquid.

Refreeze, then repeat the beating every 30 minutes or so. Do this four more times, until you have ice crystals that are loose and smooth. Eat immediately, with a shot of vodka if you like. (Any leftovers can be stored in the freezer; beat with a fork once more just before serving).

Affogato

Simple, but effective. As ever, the quality of ingredients is everything. Nescafé poured over Mr Whippy just won't cut it. This mixes creamy vanilla ice cream with searing hot, rich and bitter espresso.

{ SERVES 2 }

2 scoops good vanilla ice cream
2 freshly made single espressos

Put a scoop of vanilla ice cream into 2 bowls. Cover with hot coffee. Eat immediately.

Hot cider punch

{ SERVES 1 }

3 litres/5¼ pints good dry cider
150 g/5½ oz brown sugar
pared rind of 2 oranges
4 cloves
2 cinnamon stick, broken in half
2 star anise
big slug of Somerset cider
  brandy or Calvados

I love cider. Not that muck made from concentrate, but the proper, West Country stuff, from the likes of Julian Temperley at Burrow Hill (his Somerset cider brandy is also sublime, especially the Alchemy and 20-Year-Old stuff). I once judged the cider competition at The Royal Bath and West Show. The true pros helped me through over 300 ciders, ranging from liquid silage to apple-based bliss. Spitting out was a necessity. It was still a few weeks before I could face cider again, however good. For more information, buy James Crowden's *Ciderland* (Birlinn, 2008). This is a classic punch, served hot around Halloween or even Christmas and New Year.

In a large pan, mix the cider and sugar and slowly bring to the boil until the sugar dissolves. Add the orange rind and spices and simmer gently for 15 minutes, then leave to cool. Remove the spices and rind. Bring back to the boil, then serve in cups, adding a slug of Somerset cider brandy to each.

Hot toddy

{ SERVES 1 }

1 teaspoon clear, mild honey
25 ml/1 fl oz whisky
1–2 cloves
½ cinnamon stick
slice of lemon and juice of
  ½ lemon

This was my mother's sworn recipe to battle every sort of cold and bug. She still swears by it. As children, we made do without the whisky. But it's too good for illness alone, and is the perfect thing to warm up dreary winter's eves.

Mix the honey and whisky in a mug or heatproof glass. Add the cloves, cinnamon and lemon juice, then top up with just-off-the-boil water and stir. Add a slice of lemon and sip as soon as it doesn't burn your lips.

{ Cocktails }

As every proper person knows, there are only three cocktails worthy of serious consideration: the martini, the negroni and the bloody Mary. The rest are mere dressing, fleeting fancies and dolled-up nothings, transient concoctions made for those who hate the taste of real booze.

The martini is, of course, the greatest cocktail of them all, so simple yet so fiendishly hard to get right. It's an iconic sip, one that, in the words of Lawrence Durrell, 'fairly whistles through the rigging.' When I talk about the martini I mean dry, bone-dry, with the vermouth (Martini Extra Dry or Noilly Prat) merely hinted at, rather than sloshed in with a liberal hand. Luis Buñuel, that most fantastic of film-makers, suggested 'simply allowing a ray of sunshine to shine through a bottle of Noilly Prat before it hits the bottle of gin.' Winston Churchill thought this a step too far, instead allowing that a mere glance at the vermouth bottle while mixing one's drink is easily ample. Then there's the method of ringing up a friend in Sydney, from London, and putting the receiver next to a bottle of gin. Down in Oz, your mate should do the same with the vermouth. If these methods seem a little too extreme, then a fine mist, spritzed from a small atomiser onto the glass, does the trick. As does swilling out the glass with vermouth. You want an echo of vermouth, no more.

And a martini is always made from gin. Use vodka, and it's a vodka martini. As there's precious little else in the drink, go for the best. Beefeater, Tanqueray, Sipsmith or Plymouth are all handsome products and shine on their own. The other key ingredient is ice, lots of it. A lukewarm martini is not just an affront to good taste, but downright obscene, too. The gin or vodka must be kept in the freezer, and the glasses, too. These must be small, containing no more than three or four big sips. Any bigger, and your drink will be warm before it's finished.

As to olive versus twist of lemon, it depends on my mood. Do I want savoury, salty heft or citrus lift? One variation on the theme is a Gibson, where cocktail sticks heavy with tiny cocktail onions replace the olive or twist.

This is a short, sharp, grown-up drink. But reader beware. As James Thurber so sagaciously noted, 'One martini is alright, two are too many, three are not enough.' One last thought. Bond was wrong when he asked for shaken. It kills the smoothness, dilutes the drink too much. But then even Bond is no match for this most perfect of drinks.

Dry martini

{ SERVES 2 }

dry French vermouth
125 ml/4 fl oz gin (or vodka), near-frozen
ice
green olive or twist of lemon rind

Put 2 martini glasses in the freezer for a few hours.

Fill a small atomiser with vermouth, then spray a fine mist on the frozen martini glasses – or just wash out the glass with a jig of vermouth and pour away the excess.

Mix the gin (or vodka if you're making a vodka martini) with ice in a shaker or mixing glass, stirring about 50 times before straining into the vermouth-sprayed glass. Add an olive or a twist of lemon rind and serve immediately.

Negroni

{ SERVES 2 }

ice
1 part Martini Rosso
1 part Campari
1 part gin

The second of the great cocktails is the negroni, that ruby-red, super-bitter beauty that seems so civilised, yet packs a mighty punch. It's a drink you grow into. My grandparents adored them, but we children thought them most peculiar. And pretty disgusting, too. But like the martini, they make for a perfect apéritif, clearing the palate and fuzzing the brain in the most civilised of ways.

They also provide endless post-prandial entertainment, as I found out last year in Sicily. After a vast dinner of spaghetti with sea urchins, *arancini* and raw prawns, we made jugs of the stuff and evening turned swiftly into morning. Everyone always seemed to end up in the pool. The hangover, though, is fierce. As with the martini, ice is key, and lots of it. It offers the only respite from this boozy onslaught and, like the martini, there's no fruit juice or soda water to bring relief. Always leave for a couple of minutes after making, to mellow.

Fill 2 tumblers with ice. Add the Martini Rosso, Campari and gin. Stir, then leave for 2 minutes before drinking.

Bloody Mary

The third in the Triumvirate of great cocktails is the bloody Mary. This is lunch in a glass, the ultimate restorative, a mighty *mélange* that soothes and excites in equal measure. The tomato juice floods down the throat, lifted by the lemon, while the kick comes from the Tabasco, and depth from Worcestershire sauce. It's a drink that transcends class, equally at home in a grotty pub as it is, silver-served, in some sumptuous stately home. Horseradish has no place in the drink, needlessly sullying an already perfect party. Though many would disagree. I like a dash of fino sherry, too, and best of all, Clamato, that MSG-rich tomato drink made richer still with clam juice. It's thin and perfect when poured over crushed ice. Le Caprice, in London, makes the daddy of them all. Lemon is key, at least half per shaker, rather than the wretched, and decidedly token, pub or aeroplane sliver. Tabasco is to taste, although I see little point in a timid hand. This is supposed to shock you back into life. And shake the drink, too, with lots of ice, hard for 30 seconds. Then pour and take that first sip. The pupils dilate, the heart beats faster and last night's excess begins to clear from your brain. This is love in a glass. Bloody Mary, I bow down at your scarlet knees.

{ SERVES 1 }

ice
a very generous slug of vodka
a good glug of Tabasco
juice of ½ lemon
a few glugs of
  Worcestershire sauce
a snifter of fino sherry
a grinding of black pepper
tomato juice, or Clamato if you
  can find it, enough to fill a
  shaker three-quarters full

Put plenty of ice in a shaker. Add the vodka, followed by Tabasco, lemon juice and Worcestershire sauce, then sherry, pepper and tomato juice. Shake hard as hell for 30 seconds then serve, ice cold.

{ Slow & low }

Imagine a life of sybaritic indolence, where work is a dirty word and physical exercise, save in matters amatory, an aberration. Transport between bedroom and dining room, the two centres of your universe, is via sedan chair, carried by a sextet of Nubian dancing girls. Grapes are peeled and dropped into your mouth by blushing virgins. And an entire army of eunuchs is employed solely to squeeze lemon on to your breakfast oysters. Fun for a day or two, sure, but tiring after a while. And rather dull, too. Your flesh might be soft, tender and perfumed, but your character could be somewhat lacking.

It's the same with the more expensive cuts of meat. The chicken breast might offer snowy-white expanses of succulent flesh, but in terms of flavour, it's an also-ran compared to the thighs, wings or legs. Beef fillet has an exceptionally idle life, sitting pretty under the backbone and barely lifting a finger. So it's beautifully tender, but can fall short in terms of taste. That's not to say there's no place for a good fillet steak or plump chicken breast. Far from it. But if it's pure meaty heft you're after, then you want the cuts of meat that have done some work.

These cuts, from cheek to tail, shin to shank, are often cheaper, but tougher, too. They demand low, slow cooking, so all that connective tissue is broken down, transforming inedible collagen into soft, melting gelatin. You'll end up with great chunks of meat soft enough to cut with a spoon. This is culinary alchemy at its very finest.

This is a chapter devoted to low, slow cooking. The sort of dish that might require a little work at the start but is then left to blip and bubble away for hours. Some sit atop the hob in a barely simmering swell, others dwell in ovens no warmer than a tropical breeze.

A couple require no direct heat at all, rather the constant flow of the sweetest smoke. From proper ribs to oxtail stew, these dishes take time. But there's something deeply satisfying about taking a tough old piece of meat, lavishing it with love and low heat, and seeing it fall apart into silken strands. On the whole, these are one-pot dishes, and I can't get too excited about the differences between stew and daube, braise and casserole. To the pedant and purist, there are many, but none so important as to trouble us here. It's merely a question of kitchen semantics.

Browning of meat

Some recipes require the meat to be browned first. This does not (and never has) seal in the moisture, whatever a thousand witless TV chefs might profess. Harold McGee, author of *On Food and Cooking* (Hodder & Stoughton, 1984), has long proved this errant. No, one browns meat to get more flavour, thanks to the wonders of the Maillard reaction. Named after Louis Camille Maillard, a French physician and chemist, this is the process that creates the cooked colour and flavour of everything, from bread crust and roasted coffee to dark beers and roasted meats. On meat, it produces that wonderful caramelised crust. But you do need a high heat. Heat the oil until it smokes, then brown the meat in batches (if you overfill the pan, the meat will sweat rather than brown. Like me sitting by the pool). Drop it in, leave for about a minute, then turn and leave for the same amount of time. You want dark-brown streaks rather than insipid grey hues.

Tom's 10-alarm chili

{ SERVES 10 }

2–4 tablespoons groundnut oil
3.6 kg/8 lb shin of beef, chopped into about 10 big chunks
4 red onions, finely chopped
6 dried chipotle chillies, soaked in water for 30 minutes, then finely chopped
6 dried ancho chillies, soaked in water for 30 minutes, then finely chopped
4 habanero chillies, finely chopped
5 cloves garlic, finely chopped
3 tablespoons cumin seeds, roasted in a hot dry pan until the oils are released, then ground to a fine powder
2 big pinches of Mexican oregano (from www.coolchile.co.uk, or use European oregano if you must)
½ teaspoon cayenne pepper
½ teaspoon hot chilli powder
4 tablespoons tomato purée
Tabasco
Worcestershire sauce
1 litre/1¾ pints fresh beef stock (a decent cube will do)
grated Cheddar cheese, soured cream, crushed crackers, chopped red onion, fresh coriander leaves and tortillas or boiled white rice, to serve

Chili. One word, one million different ways with meat and spice. Forget those insipid, second-rate British versions, which are little more than mince with a sombrero and delusions of greatness. In southwestern USA, chili (note the single 'l') is less dish and more cult, art and religion all rolled into one. The perfect 'bowl of red', as it's affectionately known, is a very serious subject, with endless books devoted to its creation, and cook-offs raging non-stop. In Texas, it's a capital offence to add beans; in New Mexico, they like it pure; just meat and chilli purée mixed together, no vegetables.

'When speaking of a bowl of red, I refer to chili con carne,' wrote the late chili maestro Frank X Tolbert in his seminal *A Bowl of Red*, 'honest-to-God chili, and not the dreadful stuff masquerading as chili that is served in nine out of ten cafés.' Texas chili is my favourite, chunks of beef (or coarse ground if you must) slow-cooked with onions, garlic, Mexican oregano, freshly ground cumin seeds and chillies, fresh and dried. And remember, no beans.

Although chili sounds Mexican, and often tastes it, too, this is most certainly American. Some claim it's descended from a dish eaten by Texas pioneers on the road to California gold fields. Dried beef, chillies, suet and salt would be pounded together into a rather stodgy brick. Once on the trail, strips could be ripped off and boiled up to provide a decent dinner. Others argue that chili was a cowboy dish, using a surfeit of beef jazzed up with wild chillies picked on the open plains.

Whatever the truth, it's a poor man's dish at heart, but one best cooked in big vats. There are few finer sights than a great pot of the stuff, bubbling atop the stove. My friend James used to have a chili cook-off at his house in the week before Christmas. He favours a tomato-based, minced meat version with beans. It is pretty damned good, though, and his recipe follows mine. Just don't make it in Texas.

{ CONTINUES OVERLEAF }

The key here is the cumin and mix of fresh, dried and powdered chillies. You want spice, warmth and richness. Serve with tortillas, or a huge mound of plain white rice. Grated cheese and saltine crackers are traditional, too, and a big bowl of soured cream.

'Chili eaters is some of Your chosen people,' goes a famous chili prayer. 'We don't know why You so doggone good to us. But, Lord God, don't never think we ain't grateful for this chili we about to eat. Amen.'

Preheat the oven to 140°C/275°F/Gas 1.

Heat 2 tablespoons groundnut oil in a very large casserole over a high heat and brown the meat, in batches, then set aside.

In the same pan, add a little more oil and soften the onions over a low–medium heat for about 10 minutes, then add all the chopped chillies and garlic and cook gently for 5 minutes. Open the windows, as the fumes released are pretty eye-watering. Add more oil as you go if needed.

Add the cumin, oregano, cayenne and chilli powder and cook for a minute or so more. Then add the tomato purée and a big glug each of Tabasco and Worcestershire sauce and cook for a further 2 minutes.

Return the browned meat to the pan, stir, then add the stock. Bring just to the boil, then cover and cook in the oven for about 4–5 hours, until the meat is meltingly tender. Serve with grated cheese, soured cream, crushed crackers, chopped red onion, fresh coriander leaves and either tortillas or boiled rice.

James's 'Old Bank' chili

'It's the mix of lamb and beef as well as the Moroccan harissa paste that gives this chili its taste,' says my friend James. He gets his harissa paste from the market in Marrakech and stores it in olive oil. If Morocco is too far, then most supermarkets have a decent alternative. 'This is one of the key ingredients and gives a great flavour without going overboard on the heat. And leaving the chili overnight, once cooked, allows the magic to happen.' The only thing I'd disagree with is his advice about serving it with brown rice. In my view, this is best left to the hippies. But it's his recipe, and damned fine it is, too. You can freeze any you don't eat.

Heat 2 tablespoons olive oil in a frying pan, add the chillies, onions, garlic and peppers and cook until soft.

Heat the remaining olive oil in a very large casserole over a high heat and brown all the mince, in batches. Add more oil as you go if needed. Return all the mince to the pan. Add the chilli and onion mixture, then add half the wine and all the canned tomatoes, passata, harissa paste and Worcestershire sauce. Turn the heat right down and simmer, uncovered, stirring occasionally, for 1 hour.

Add the kidney beans and the rest of the wine and leave to simmer for another hour, or until the chili is the required consistency. If it is too dry, add more passata and red wine (you can never have enough). If too wet, keep simmering. Taste for salt and chili and adjust accordingly, adding a little more harissa paste if you like.

Leave the chili to sit overnight, covered, in the fridge: this lets the flavours meld together into something amazing. The next day, reheat the chili until hot through and serve with soured cream, grated Cheddar and boiled brown rice.

{ SERVES 10 }

4 tablespoons olive oil

5–10 bird's-eye chillies, finely chopped

3 big white onions, finely chopped

cloves from 1 head of garlic, finely chopped

3 red peppers, deseeded and finely chopped

1 kg/2 lb 2 oz minced beef

1 kg/2 lb 2 oz minced lamb

75 cl bottle of punchy red wine

3 x 400 g cans chopped tomatoes

1.4 litres/2½ pints tomato passata

2 tablespoons harissa chilli paste, or more, to taste

3 tablespoons Worcestershire sauce

3 x 400 g cans red kidney beans, drained and rinsed

sea salt

soured cream, grated Cheddar and boiled brown rice to serve

Pot-au-feu

{ SERVES 8 }

900 g/2 lb shin of beef, in one piece
900 g/2 lb silverside of beef (or topside)
1 x 600 g/1 lb 5 oz oxtail, cut into thick pieces
6 carrots, roughly chopped
4 leeks, white and light-green parts only, roughly chopped
2 celery stalks, roughly chopped
3 large onions, halved, one half studded with 3 cloves
1 head of garlic, left whole
2 tomatoes, halved
6 peppercorns
1 bouquet garni (2 bay leaves, 1 sprig of celery leaves, 3 sprigs of thyme, 4 parsley leaves, stalks and, if possible, roots, too – all tied together in a piece of cheesecloth)
2 beef marrowbones (optional) – get the butcher to saw them in half or quarter them, depending on the size of your pan
sea salt and freshly ground black pepper

If ever three words were imbued with Gallic history, pride and delight, they are *pot-au-feu*. For this is no mere stew, rather a cornerstone of French cuisine, a dish that spans regions and classes like some meat-scented Colossus. 'In France,' wrote no lesser an authority than Auguste Escoffier, 'the *pot-au-feu* is the symbol of family life… A good *pot-au-feu* will always be a comfortable and thoroughly bourgeois dish that nothing may dethrone.' Revolutionary, writer and all-round renaissance man the Comte de Mirabeau went one step further. 'The foundation of empires,' he proclaimed proudly.

Pot-au-feu's origins lie in the ever-simmering soup pot, traditionally found at the back of most French kitchens, into which bones, vegetables and scraps of meat would be thrown. It would be continually eaten and replenished. And if the family had money, pieces of meat would be added.

There are myriad versions of *pot-au-feu* in France, each region united in the certainty that its version is the only one of any merit. As the name suggests, though, this is just a pot over the fire and open to all manner of interpretation. In the Languedoc, there's beef, bacon and cabbage. Up near the Pyrenees, by Tarn, a stuffed bird is added. (Some favour stuffed goose neck, others raw ham, salt pork, confit duck, mutton, goose and cabbage). The key is mixing different flavours and textures: gelatinous, fatty and lean. The broth is drunk first, and the meat served with mustard, pickles, horseradish and pickled onions. You will need a very big pot, for this is a feast, and best served to a big table of ravenous guests.

Place both pieces of beef and the oxtail in a large enamelled or stainless-steel pan or stockpot and cover with cold water. Bring slowly to the boil, then simmer until scum forms and skim off the scum. Continue simmering and repeating the skimming for 10 minutes, until the scum changes from mucky grey to white froth. Tip away the water, return the beef and oxtail to the pan and cover with fresh cold water.

Add the carrots, leeks, celery, onions, garlic, tomatoes, peppercorns and bouquet garni and bring to the boil. Turn down to the merest simmer, cover with a lid (leaving a small gap) and simmer gently for 2 hours. Add the marrowbones and simmer gently for a further 1–1½ hours.

Allow to cool, then skim off any excess fat. Strain the broth into a clean pan and bring back to the boil. Season to taste. Pour over slices of baguette in bowls and top with a sprinkling of grated Gruyère. Scoop out the cooked marrow and add to the bouillon along with the soft garlic cloves, discarding the papery skins.

Serve the meat and vegetables with a pile of good salt, the mustards, cornichons, pickled onions and horseradish.

To serve
1 baguette, sliced
175–200 g/6–7 oz
  Gruyère, grated
a small bowl of sea salt
Dijon mustard
English mustard
cornichons
small pickled onions
freshly grated horseradish

Slow & low

Boeuf en daube

I remember this dish from Virginia Woolf's *To the Lighthouse*. Actually, it's about all I remember from the book, the '…. exquisite scent of olive and oil and juice' rising from the dish as the top was taken off. It took Mrs Ramsay's maid, Mildred, three days to cook, although this seems a touch excessive. Overnight in the marinade, I suppose, then a few hours in a low oven. It's always better the next day anyway. But the ever-anxious hostess's frets about it being spoiled, thanks to the guests coming in late, are unfounded. This daube improves as it's heated and cooled down, and is also wonderful cold. Cooked properly, this is robust enough to deal with all manner of tardy diners.

Put the beef in a non-reactive dish and cover with the marinade ingredients. Cover with cling film and refrigerate overnight. When you are ready to cook the daube, preheat the oven to 140°C/275°F/Gas 1. Lift the beef out of the marinade and drain. Strain the marinade into a jug. Heat the oil in a large heavy-bottomed casserole over a high heat and brown the meat on both sides. Remove and set aside.

In the same casserole, cook the bacon and pork rinds (if using) over a medium–high heat until crisp; remove and set aside. Lay half the bacon and rinds in the casserole. Add the carrots, onions, parsley, bay leaf, garlic, orange rind and remaining bacon. Put the beef on top and pour over the reserved marinade and red wine to cover, followed by the remaining rinds and the tomatoes. Bring to the boil, cover with foil and a tight lid and bake for 2½–3 hours until tender.

If you can, leave to cool, skim off the fat, remove the parsley stalks and bay leaves and leave in the fridge, covered, overnight. Reheat thoroughly the next day, adding the black olives. If the sauce seems thin, lift out the meat and vegetables with a slotted spoon and keep warm while you boil the sauce for 5–10 minutes to thicken. Serve the daube with cooked noodles doused in olive oil, or plain rice.

{ **SERVES 6** }

1.3 kg/3 lb top rump of beef or shin, cut into 'squares', in the words of Elizabeth David, 'the size of half a postcard' and about 1 cm/½ inch thick
2 tablespoons olive oil
5 rashers unsmoked streaky bacon, cut into small pieces
85 g/3 oz fresh pork rinds (optional)
3 carrots, cut into 1 cm/½ inch slices
3 onions, finely chopped
4 parsley stalks
1 bay leaf
2 cloves garlic, bruised
small strip of pared orange rind
½ x 75 cl bottle of good red wine
4 tomatoes, skinned, deseeded and sliced
handful of good black olives, pitted
cooked noodles or white rice, to serve

For the marinade

½ x 75 cl bottle of good red wine
2 tablespoons olive oil
a few sprigs of thyme
4 cloves garlic, bruised
1–2 sprigs of rosemary
2 bay leaves
5 black peppercorns, crushed

Slow & low

Boeuf Bourguignon

{ SERVES 4 }

4 tablespoons olive oil
1 small onion, roughly chopped
8 cloves garlic, bruised with back of knife
1 large carrot, roughly chopped
2 celery stalks, roughly chopped
4 sprigs of thyme
2 bay leaves
75cl bottle of decent red Burgundy (well, something around the £10 mark)
250 ml/9 fl oz beef stock (best you can find, although cubes are just about OK)
50 g/1¾ oz butter
100 g/3½ oz smoked lardons or smoked streaky bacon, chopped into small pieces
150 g/5½ oz button mushrooms
24 button/pearl onions, peeled (plunge into boiling water for a minute first), or 400 g/14 oz small shallots
sea salt and freshly ground black pepper
2 tablespoons plain flour
1 kg/2 lb 2 oz topside of beef, fat left on and cut into largish chunks, the size of a small lady's fist

There's no point beating around the bush. Making this rich, wonderful Burgundian classic takes time. And the ingredients look daunting. There are mushrooms, lardons, pearl onions and beef, all needing to be browned. There are sauces to reduce and strain, trotters to be hewn in half, fat to be skimmed. But none of it actually requires masses of skill. It takes a good few hours to prepare, and is best eaten the next day.

I once cooked it for 30 people, and the house stank of browned everything for days afterwards. But if you enjoy cooking, you'll love this. Arm yourself with a glass of wine, whack on some Allman Brothers and spend an afternoon soaked in good Burgundy.

As to ingredients, I like topside as it has a good amount of fat and suits slow cooking. You could use shin, too. And track down the tiny pearl onions. Any greengrocer worth his, well, onions, will have them. The pig's trotter is optional, but your butcher should give you one for free – get him or her to split it, and if you're worried about it fitting it into your pot, ask for it to be cut in half crossways. The trotter adds a wonderful gelatinous wobble to the dish.

Heat 2 tablespoons of oil in a frying pan, add the onion and soften over a medium heat for 5 minutes. Add the garlic, carrot and celery and slightly caramelise, without burning.

Add the thyme and bay leaves, then pour in the wine. Bring to the boil and ignite the wine (stand well back and watch it like a hawk; pull it off the heat if you feel it burns for too long). Once the flame has gone, add the stock and turn down the heat. Simmer for 30 minutes, or until reduced by half. Strain the liquid into a large jug and set aside. Discard the vegetables.

Preheat the oven to 140°C/275°F/Gas 1. Melt the butter and remaining olive oil in a large heavy-bottomed casserole over a medium–high heat. Fry the lardons or bacon until crisp, then set aside. Brown the mushrooms in the same pan, then remove, add more oil if necessary, and brown the pearl onions. Scrape the bottom of the pan occasionally to remove any crusty bits.

Season the flour. Roll the beef in the flour and brown in batches in more oil if necessary; set aside. Do the same with the pig's trotter until burnished. Leave the trotter in the pot, pour out any excess fat and return the bacon, mushrooms, pearl onions and beef to the pan. Turn up the heat and deglaze the pan with the Cognac. Ignite, let it burn out, then pour in the sauce you made earlier. Bring to a simmer and skim.

Cover with a lid and put the casserole in the oven for 3–3½ hours, or until the beef is tender.

Remove and discard the trotter. Check the seasoning and leave to cool. Remove any fat from the top of the casserole. If possible, leave in the fridge overnight to ensure a polite exchange of flavours. Reheat thoroughly, add the lemon juice and parsley, stir in the Dijon mustard and serve with mashed potatoes.

1 pig's trotter, split lengthways (optional)
75 ml/3 fl oz Cognac
juice of ½ lemon
1 tablespoon finely chopped flat-leaf parsley
1 tablespoon Dijon mustard

Home-made salt beef

{ SERVES 8 }

2.5 kg/5 lb 8 oz rolled brisket
2 carrots, roughly chopped
2 onions, roughly chopped
1 celery stalk, roughly chopped
4 cloves garlic
1 bouquet garni (2 bay leaves, 1 sprig of celery leaves, 3 sprigs of thyme, 4 parsley leaves, stalks and, if possible, roots, too – all tied together in a piece of cheesecloth)
boiled potatoes, to serve
freshly grated horseradish, to serve

For the brine
700 g/1 lb 9 oz rock salt
300 g/10½ oz demerara sugar
1 dried habanero chilli (optional)
3 small dried chillies
3 bay leaves
10 black peppercorns
2 star anise
2 cloves
2 sprigs of thyme
5 cloves garlic
25 g/1 oz Prague Powder No 1 (this is the saltpetre, and optional)

This is an epic recipe, but it's more *Independence Day* than *Odyssey* as the action takes place over about eight or so days. Home-made salt beef is miles removed from the bland, chewy, pre-sliced stuff you get in the shops. It's rich and luscious, scented with spices and falls apart in great chunks.

As to its history, there are the usual debates, arguments and polite exchanges of opinion. A recipe for pickled beef, in Robert May's *The Accomplisht Cook*, was published in 1660. And the Irish were responsible for creating the lucrative export market right up until the 19th century, when British-canned South American beef (far cheaper) took over.

Wherever there was beef, there would have been a preserved version. In the days before refrigeration, the salting of meat was essential. But for me, salt beef is associated with the food of the Ashkenazi Jews of Central and Eastern Europe. Thanks in part to *kashruth*, the strict Jewish dietary laws, only the tough forequarters, away from the rump, could be used. And they had to be cooked within 72 hours of slaughter. Without time to hang and tenderise, salting and slow cooking was the best way to turn tough meat into stuff that could be eaten with a spoon. The East and West End of London, along with most of New York, used to be packed with salt-beef bars. Now, only a few remain, the best of which is the Brass Rail at Selfridges.

To get the proper pink tinge, saltpetre is essential. But if you can't get hold of it, worry not, as the flavour remains the same. Either eat it hot, carved into thick slices, with horseradish and boiled potatoes or cold, sliced very thinly, on rye bread, slathered with English mustard.

As to the pickling receptacle, a big strong bag is most practical. Try Lakeland (www.lakeland.co.uk), the Mecca for all kitchen supplies. I've also used a washing-up bowl. Make sure it fits in the fridge and the liquid completely covers the meat.

To make the brine, put all the ingredients into a large pot with 4 litres/7 pints water, bring to the boil, then simmer for 4 minutes. Turn off the heat and allow to cool completely.

Put the beef into a non-metallic bowl (or strong, clean plastic bag or washing-up bowl), cover with brine (using a plate to weight down if necessary) and cover with cling film. Leave in the fridge for about 7 days, turning every day.

Rinse the beef and soak overnight in fresh water.

Discard the soaking water and put the beef into a pot with the carrots, onions, celery, garlic and bouquet garni. Cover with fresh water, bring to the boil and simmer gently, covered, for 2–2½ hours, or until very tender. Remove the bouquet garni and discard along with the liquid and veg. Serve hot, with boiled potatoes and horseradish, or cold, with mustard.

Carbonade flamande

{ SERVES 6 }

2–2½ tablespoons beef dripping
4 onions, thinly sliced
25 g/1 oz plain flour
2 teaspoons English mustard powder
salt and freshly ground black pepper
1 kg/2 lb 2 oz stewing steak, cut into 4 cm/1½ inch cubes
2 tablespoons red-wine vinegar
350 ml/12 fl oz Belgian blond beer
100 ml/3½ fl oz beef stock
1 tablespoon brown sugar
1 bouquet garni (2 bay leaves, 1 sprig of celery leaves, 3 sprigs of thyme, 4 parsley leaves, stalks and, if possible, roots, too – all tied together in a piece of cheesecloth)
1 tablespoon Dijon mustard
mashed potatoes, to serve

I wouldn't want to be a Belgian. Tintin was always inferior to Asterix, and Poirot dreamt up by an English Dame. OK, so Jean-Claude Van Damme is a kick-ass legend. And they're good with mussels, chips and beers. And feeding those great bloated Eurocrats who infect the EU. But please don't bang on about their chocolates. They all taste the same – overbearing and smugly rich. Still, their beer's alright. Choose a decent one for this dish, something with a bite of bitter. A good Abbey Blond beer will work.

As to the name, it's actually Spanish in origin and means 'grilled over coals'. Whereas this is a slow-cooked stew. Belgians, eh? Still, it's a cracking good stew.

Preheat the oven to 150°C/300°F/Gas 2. Heat 1 tablespoon of the dripping in a heavy-based frying pan and fry the onions until lightly coloured but not brown. Lift out with a slotted spoon and transfer to a shallow lidded casserole.

In a shallow bowl, combine the flour with the mustard powder, salt and pepper and toss the meat in this to coat.

Heat the remaining dripping in the frying pan over a high heat. Brown the meat in batches and transfer to the casserole.

Add the vinegar, beer and stock to the frying pan with the sugar and bouquet garni. Season to taste and stir until simmering, scraping any residue from the bottom of the pan.

Pour the sauce over the meat and onions, cover tightly and cook in the oven for 3 hours, or until very tender.

Remove the bouquet garni and stir in the Dijon mustard. Serve with mashed potatoes.

Ragù alla Bolognese

The standard British spaghetti Bolognese is a relentlessly gloomy affair. Take one over-the-hill onion, and maul, before dumping into searing vegetable oil and cooking until the edges are burnt and bitter and the centre resolutely hard. Do the same to a couple of cloves of garlic, then throw in a packet or two of economy mince, all grey and gristly. And overcook. Remember to overload the pan, so the meat boils rather than browns. Only then will you turn the beef into the rubbery, bovine pellets that are so essential to this hateful dish. Seasonings come next, a splodge of ketchup, an over-diluted stock cube and a dusty handful of impotent dried herbs. Boil indiscriminately for 20 minutes, then mix with a glut of overcooked, claggy pasta. Finish with a dusting of vomit-scented 'Parmesan style' powder and serve with a grimace. An insipid car crash of a creation, this is food as lowest common denominator, little more than barely edible depression.

Of course, spaghetti Bolognese is one of those Frankenstein's monster sort of beasts, where a great European regional dish (in this case, the *ragù alla Bolognese*) sets off abroad and returns almost unrecognisable with new accent, name and nose job. 'When the Italians emigrated to the USA, just before the Great War, they'd bring with them foods that would last the journey, long bundles of spaghetti and the like,' says the Queen of Italian gastronomy Anna del Conte. 'And when they arrived, they added meat to the classic tomato sauce. So spaghetti Bolognese was born, and the American invention eventually made it over to England, and London's Soho in particular.' It became so popular that it even returned to parts of Italy.

{ CONTINUES OVERLEAF }

{ SERVES 6 }

25 g/1 oz butter
2 tablespoons olive oil
1 onion, finely chopped
1 carrot, finely chopped
1 celery stalk, finely chopped
2 cloves garlic, finely chopped
1 bouquet garni (2 bay leaves, 1 sprig of celery leaves, 3 sprigs of thyme, 4 parsley leaves, stalks and, if possible, roots, too – all tied together in a piece of cheesecloth)
75 g/3 oz chicken livers, rinsed, trimmed and finely chopped
125 g/4½ oz pancetta or unsmoked bacon, finely chopped
350 g/12 oz beef, pork or veal mince, or a mixture
300 ml/10 fl oz red wine
sea salt and freshly ground black pepper
4 tablespoons tomato purée
300 ml/10 fl oz fresh beef stock
150 ml/5 fl oz double cream
tagliatelle, to serve
freshly grated Parmesan, to serve

The most elegant and perceptive of women, I'm surprised Anna can still look me in the eye, after an incident where I managed to soak her exquisite cashmere twin set in greasy muck. She was sitting at a table with my co-presenter Matthew Fort, during a recording of *Market Kitchen* for what was then UKTV Food. While I was gurning at the camera, I heard Matthew say something particularly irritating (probably some nonsense about not seasoning your steak before cooking, or how rusk in a sausage is an aberration). So I grabbed the nearest projectile, a vast red chilli, and, not actually looking at my target, hurled it with all my might. My aim, alas, was far from true and the pungent pod flew hard into a plate of caponata. I looked up to see Anna dripping in oil and vinegar. She was not amused.

But back to the real *ragù*. Over in Bologna, that great and meaty Italian city, the *ragù* would be served with fresh tagliatelle, those thickish ribbons a perfect partner to the rich, slow-cooked meat sauce. But pappardelle, penne rigate and farfalle are all well suited, too, allowing the sauce to stick and nestle in every nook and groove.

And the sauce itself? Well, as ever in matters of European gastronomy, it depends upon whom you ask. Some swear by the addition of tomatoes, while others denounce their inclusion as grotesque. One family might include a good whack of milk or cream for extra smoothness. Another would curse the very thought. Beef and veal are standard, but recipes also include chicken livers, Parma ham, fresh pork, lardo, even game. This is a rich, hefty, slow-cooked sauce, and not only will each region have its own version, but each street and house. Needless to say, the 'best' recipe is always their own. Most recipes start with finely chopped celery, carrots and onions, but not all. The key is the slow, low cook, which transforms tough cuts into silken strands of unctuous delight.

Over the years, I've trawled through many a recipe, and tried them all. Chicken liver, finely chopped, adds not only luscious texture, but real depth of flavour, too. Milk or cream provides lactic bite, and pancetta or prosciutto crudo still more layers of taste. This makes a blissfully rich *ragù*. And one to banish all thoughts of the horrific spag Bol to the culinary rubbish dump for ever.

Heat the butter and oil in a deep saucepan over a medium heat. Add the vegetables, garlic and bouquet garni and fry until they soften and brown lightly. Add the livers and cook until pink – about 2 minutes. Add the pancetta and minced meat and fry until the meat colours. Add the wine, simmer until it evaporates, then add seasoning, the tomato purée and a little of the stock. Cook slowly, covered, stirring occasionally and gradually adding more stock.

After 1½ hours, stir in the cream and continue to cook, uncovered, until reduced – about another hour.

Remove the bouquet garni. Cook the tagliatelle and serve with the Bolognese and lots of freshly grated Parmesan.

Oxtail stew

{ SERVES 4 }

1.25 kg/2 lb 12 oz oxtail, cut into rounds, excess fat removed
sea salt and freshly ground black pepper
1 teaspoon chilli powder
1 teaspoon English mustard powder
2 tablespoons plain flour
2 tablespoons olive oil
60 g/2¼ oz butter
2 carrots, roughly chopped
2 onions, roughly chopped
8 closed-cap mushrooms, roughly chopped
4 cloves garlic, thinly sliced
4 sprigs of thyme
4 bay leaves
75 cl bottle of punchy red wine such as Rioja or Châteauneuf-du-Pape
1 tablespoon Worcestershire sauce
1 tablespoon Dijon mustard
handful of parsley, roughly chopped

Some of the sweetest meat comes from the cow's tail; wobbling, slightly gelatinous chunks that are the very essence of proper winter food. This is the hale and hearty made flesh. As with so many once-cheap ingredients (pork belly, lamb shanks, pig's cheek), they become trendy, get a taste for Balenciaga and the price rockets. Still, this is a rich, serious dish, spiked with a touch of chilli and mustard, that's best served slopped all over buttery mashed potatoes. Once cooked, leave it in the fridge, covered, overnight. Then reheat the next day.

Soak the oxtail in salted water, covered in the fridge, for a couple of hours. Drain, put into a pan of fresh, unsalted water and bring to the boil. Reduce the heat and simmer for 15 minutes, then remove from the heat and leave to cool. Pat dry. Preheat the oven to 150°C/300°F/Gas 2.

Mix the chilli and mustard powders in a plastic zip-seal bag with the flour, salt and pepper. Drop in the oxtail and shake until covered. In a large casserole, heat the oil and butter over a high heat until foaming, then brown the oxtail in batches. Remove the oxtail and set aside. Reduce the heat slightly and brown the carrots, onions and mushrooms. When they are browned, add the garlic, thyme and bay.

Put the oxtail back in the casserole. Add the wine and Worcestershire sauce, season, then bring to the boil and skim off any fat. Cover the casserole and put it into the oven for 3 hours, or until the meat is very tender.

Lift the oxtail onto a plate, pull the meat off the bones and add back to the stew. Leave overnight in the fridge, covered. The next day, remove the layer of fat from the top of the casserole. Reheat thoroughly until piping hot, stir in the mustard and parsley and serve with mashed potatoes.

Braised ox cheeks

Like oxtail, ox cheek was once a cheap, dowdy, resolutely unglamorous cut, but has ascended to the A-list. And I can see why. Cooked slowly, these cheeks, with all that hard-working connective fibre, break down into the most luscious strands. They have a sublime richness and should be eaten with a spoon, from a bowl.

Season the flour. Chop each ox cheek into 4–6 pieces, then dust them with the seasoned flour. Heat the oil in a frying pan over a high heat and brown the meat in batches. Transfer the meat to a large saucepan or flameproof casserole. Deglaze the frying pan with a splash of the beer and pour it over the meat.

Add the celery, leek and carrots to the casserole and cover with the stock. Pour in the Worcestershire sauce and the rest of the beer. Bring to the boil, then reduce the heat and simmer gently for about 1½ hours, or until the meat is tender and falling apart.

Remove the meat from the casserole and set aside. Boil the liquid, uncovered, until it has thickened slightly: about 20 minutes. Return the ox cheeks to the gravy to heat them through, then serve in a bowl with mashed potatoes and the gravy.

{ SERVES 4 }

2 tablespoons plain flour
sea salt and freshly ground black pepper
2 ox cheeks, about 300–400 g/ 10½–14 oz each (ask your butcher to remove the skin and fat)
1 tablespoon vegetable oil
200 ml/7 fl oz stout or London porter
2 celery stalks, cut into chunky matchstick lengths
1 leek, halved and sliced
2 carrots, roughly chopped
1 litre/1¾ pints chicken stock
1 tablespoon Worcestershire sauce
mashed potatoes, to serve

Oxtail consommé (& Bullshot)

{ SERVES 4–6 }

1 oxtail, about 600 g/1 lb 5 oz, cut into 4 pieces, excess fat removed
2 onions, halved lengthways, topped and tailed but not peeled
2 carrots, roughly chopped
4 celery stalks, roughly chopped
2 bay leaves
6 black peppercorns
handful of parsley stalks
200 ml/7 fl oz dry white wine
good splash of fino or manzanilla sherry, to serve

I have an obsession with consommés, those clear, glittering soups that pack a mighty flavour punch. They're what my wife would call 'medicinal eating', the sort of food that leaves you glowing with health and feeling rather smug. It's becoming increasingly difficult to find a good canned consommé. Sainsbury's did a good version, but it seems it has moved on to the great recycling plant in the sky. Leaving me high and dry. Thank God, then, for Baxter's and Lusty's. Their beef consommés are crackers. But this recipe is very easy.

It also makes the base for a Bullshot. Heat the consommé and mix with Worcestershire sauce, Tabasco and the juice of half a lemon, then pour into glasses and mix with a measure of vodka. In summer, drink over ice.

Preheat the oven to 240°C/475°F/Gas 9. Put the oxtail and onions on a baking tray. Brown in the oven for 20 minutes.

Put the browned meat and onions into a big pot with the carrots, celery, bay leaves, peppercorns and parsley stalks. Cover with about 2 litres/3½ pints water (filtered if possible) and the wine. Bring to the boil, skim, then turn the heat down so there is the occasional blip rather than constant bubbling; do not let it boil.

Cook for about 4 hours, until the oxtail is very tender, topping up the water if need be. Strain into a bowl (reserving some shards of oxtail meat), cool and put into the fridge overnight. It should set into a mass of gleaming brown jelly. Skim off the fat, then put the jelly into a pan and gently reheat. Taste and adjust the seasoning. Ladle into serving bowls with a few nuggets of meat and add a dash of sherry to taste.

Braised venison

Venison's a highly underrated meat and can range from the majestically rich (a well-hung red deer, say) to the subtle and sweet (muntjac, perhaps the finest of them all). Farmed deer are of a decent quality, and are probably the easiest to find in supermarkets. This recipe comes from my late step-mother Rose.

To make the marinade, put all the ingredients into a pan, bring to the boil and simmer for 3 minutes. Allow to cool.

Put the venison into a deep non-reactive bowl and cover with the marinade. Cover and marinate in the fridge for at least 24 hours (48 even better), turning occasionally.

Preheat the oven to 170°C/325°F/Gas 3. Remove the venison from the marinade and wipe dry with kitchen paper. Strain the marinade (reserving the bouquet garni) and set aside.

Heat the dripping in a large heavy-bottomed pan over a high heat and brown the meat all over. Remove and set aside. Reduce the heat slightly and in the same pan brown the onions, carrots and celery. Put the venison back in the pan, along with the bouquet garni, strained marinade and stock. Season, bring to the boil, then put into the oven for 2½–3 hours, until cooked and meltingly tender.

Transfer the venison to a carving board and slice. Strain the cooking liquid into a clean pan and skim, then add redcurrant jelly and whisk in the kneaded butter. Reduce by half, stir in the cream, then pour over the sliced venison. Serve with spiced red cabbage and mashed potatoes.

{ SERVES 4 }

1.3 kg/3 lb haunch of venison
1 tablespoon dripping, lard or goose fat
2 onions, finely chopped
2 carrots, finely chopped
2 celery stalks, finely chopped
300 ml/10 fl oz chicken stock (cube OK)
1 teaspoon redcurrant jelly
kneaded butter (mix 20 g/¾ oz butter with 20 g/¾ oz plain flour and knead until smooth)
2–3 tablespoons double cream

For the marinade
1 large onion, thinly sliced
1 large carrot, thinly sliced
1 celery stalk, thinly sliced
1 clove garlic
6 peppercorns
2 tablespoons olive oil
1 bouquet garni (2 bay leaves, 1 sprig of celery leaves, 3 sprigs of thyme, 4 parsley leaves, stalks and, if possible, roots, too – all tied together in a piece of cheesecloth)
300 ml/10 fl oz red wine
2 tablespoons red-wine vinegar
2 pieces of pared rind from an unwaxed lemon, as long as a little finger, chopped
pared rind of 1 orange
6 juniper berries, crushed

Proper ribs

{ SERVES 4 }

I hadn't tasted proper ribs – the real, bone-sucking beauties, rather than those dried-up, mealy-mouthed twigs that pass for ribs over here – until about seven years ago. I was a judge, one of many, at the Jack Daniel's Invitational Barbecue competition in Lynchburg, Tennessee. Two days were spent learning the ins and outs of professional pit judging – what garnishes were acceptable (green-leaf lettuce, common curly parsley and coriander), how to tell if ribs were perfectly done ('When eating a properly cooked rib, the meat should come off the bone with very little effort and only where you bite into it should the meat be removed') and how to mark my meat (appearance, taste and tenderness, one worst, nine impossibly brilliant). Before standing to take my oath to 'truth, justice, excellence in barbecue and the American way of life.' With my right hand aloft, my eyes raised towards heaven.

Because in the south and southeast of America, barbecue does not mean abusing some perfectly innocent burger over a roaring flame. Real 'que' is all about slow and low. Grilling is cooking over a direct heat. Barbecuing sees tough cuts of beef and pork smoked over an indirect heat for hours, until all those connective tissues are broken down into lusciously soft gelatin. As Lolis Eric Elie writes in *Smokestack Lightning* (Ten Speed Press, 2005) the 'que' heads '... worship their own gods, they speak their own language and they think that the ability to distinguish a brisket from a butt is no less basic to a civilised existence than are lounge chairs and chilled beer'.

Once you're bitten by the bug, things get complicated pretty quickly. Oak or hickory, apple or cherry? Some pit masters like wet rubs, others dry. Texans love brisket, yet barbecue is predominantly pork – whole or hewn into various cuts. And as for the sauces... things get real fun here. In the west of North Carolina, pork shoulder is cooked over hickory or oak, then chopped or sliced and served with

{ CONTINUES OVERLEAF }

{ SERVES 4–6 }

500 ml/18 fl oz cider vinegar

2 kg/4 lb 8 oz baby back pork ribs

For the dry rub

2 tablespoons hot paprika

2 tablespoons ground black pepper

2 tablespoons sea salt

1 teaspoon cayenne pepper

4 tablespoons muscovado sugar

2 tablespoons garlic powder

2 tablespoons onion powder

For the sauce

25 g/1 oz butter

1 onion, finely chopped

4 cloves garlic, finely chopped

125 ml/4 fl oz Bourbon

175 ml/6 fl oz tomato ketchup

70 g/2½ oz dark brown sugar

175 ml/6 fl oz cider vinegar

1½ teaspoons English mustard powder

1 tablespoon soy sauce

2 teaspoons honey

1 tablespoon lemon juice

1 teaspoon chilli powder

½ teaspoon cayenne pepper

1 tablespoon Worcestershire sauce

½ teaspoon Tabasco

a tomato-based sauce. On the eastern side of the same state, barbecue means whole hog with a vinegar and pepper-spiked dressing. As Calvin Trillin wryly points out, 'Americans argue not just about whose barbecue is second-best, but even what barbecue is about.'

I use a Bradley Smoker for my ribs, a home smoker about the size of a mini bar. But the recipe below can be done in a classic kettle grill, too.

Mix 9 litres/16 pints water with the 500 ml/18 fl oz vinegar, then soak the ribs in this mixture, covered and in the fridge, for 1 hour. Drain and dry with kitchen paper.

For the dry rub, mix all the ingredients together, then rub the mixture into the ribs (reserving the rest for later). Wrap in foil and leave in the fridge overnight.

To make the sauce, melt the butter in a saucepan over a medium heat and soften the onion and garlic. Add the Bourbon, then all the other ingredients and cook at a gentle simmer for 30 minutes. Cover and set aside.

If using a Bradley Smoker, heat to 210°F, and use some hickory briquettes. Cook the ribs, wrapped in foil, on the top shelf for 1½ hours, then move to the bottom shelf for another 1½ hours. Take the ribs out and rub with the remaining dry rub, then cook on the top shelf for a further 1 hour and 45 minutes. Unwrap the foil, baste the ribs with sauce, rewrap and cook on the bottom shelf for a further 45 minutes.

If using a kettle barbecue, pile charcoal on one side of the base of the barbecue and put an old small roasting tin filled with water on a couple of bricks on the other side. Light the charcoal and heat until the coals are white-hot.

Sit the ribs, wrapped in the foil, on a rack over the water. Cover the barbecue with a lid, with the smoke holes half open. Use these holes to regulate the temperature, so when it begins to drop close the vents and open them when it gets very hot. Cook for 3 hours – you will need to top up the charcoal about every 40–60 minutes.

Rub the ribs with the remaining spice rub, rewrap in the foil and return to the barbecue for another 2–3 hours, until tender, topping up the charcoal from time to time. An hour before the end of the cooking time, open the foil and baste the ribs with the sauce.

When ready, the ribs should pull apart easily; the meat should not be falling off the bone but will come off cleanly when tugged by the teeth.

Pulled pork

A classic barbecue dish, taking a cheap shoulder of pork and cooking it at a low heat for hours, until the meat can be cut with a spoon. In barbecue joints in the US, it's served with cheap white bread. The sauce is from east Carolina, spiked with vinegar and pepper, and cuts through the rich meat.

Mix all the ingredients for the dry rub and massage half the mixture into the pork. Wrap the pork in cling film and leave in the fridge overnight.

The next day, remove the pork from the fridge, massage with the remaining dry rub and let the pork come to room temperature.

If using a Bradley Smoker, heat to 200°F and cook the pork on one shelf from the bottom for 8 hours.

If using a kettle barbecue, soak 1½ x 450 g packs of maple woodchips in a bucket of cold water as directed on the pack. Pile charcoal on one side of the base of the barbecue and put an old small roasting tin filled with cold water on a couple of bricks on the other side. Light the charcoal and leave until the coals are white. Sit the pork on foil with the edges folded up, then put it on the floating shelf (the shelf that is attached inside the lid) over the water, with a digital meat thermometer set to 'pork' inserted into the meat (follow the manufacturer's instructions for using the

{ CONTINUES OVERLEAF }

{ SERVES 6 }

1.8–2.3 kg/4–5 lb rolled shoulder of pork

For the dry rub
25 g/1 oz freshly ground black pepper
25 g/1 oz hot paprika
25 g/1 oz demerara sugar
2 tablespoons sea salt
2 teaspoons dry mustard powder
2 teaspoons cayenne pepper
2 teaspoons celery salt

For the east Carolina vinegar sauce
450 ml/16 fl oz cider vinegar
2 tablespoons brown sugar
2 teaspoons sea salt
1 teaspoon freshly ground black pepper
2 teaspoons hot chilli flakes or cayenne pepper

thermometer). Scoop out a handful of soaked woodchips, add to the top of coals and quickly shut the lid, with the smoke holes half open (see page 175). After 40 minutes, top up with more charcoal. After a further 40–60 minutes, top up with more charcoal and a handful of drained woodchips. Keep the barbecue lid open for as short a time as possible so you don't lose heat or smoke. Cook for at least 6 hours (8 or 9 is better), checking every 40 minutes or so to ensure the heat is sufficient – top up with more charcoal when necessary.

Take out the pork and allow to cool slightly. Put all the ingredients for the sauce in a pan and heat gently, stirring, for long enough to dissolve the sugar. Serve with the meat.

Petit salé aux lentilles

A hale and hearty northern French dish, this is a recipe inspired by my friend Bill Knott, a fine cook and food writer. Sunday lunch at his house has been known to stretch well into Monday. Conversation may ebb and flow, but the stream of wine is continuous. This is also rather good cold.

Chop half the garlic into thick slivers and secrete them about the pork. Put the pork in a non-reactive container (or a strong plastic bag) and cover with sea salt. Add most of the thyme and scrunch it into the salt. Cover and leave in the fridge for 48–72 hours, turning when you remember.

Rinse the pork well in cold water. Put it in a pan, cover with cold water and bring to a very gentle simmer. Add the bay and peppercorns and simmer, lid on, for 1½–2 hours over a low heat, until nearly tender, skimming occasionally. When the pork is cooked, remove it and strain and reserve the broth. When the meat is cool, remove the rib bones.

Heat the goose fat or olive oil in a big saucepan over a medium heat, then add the onions, carrots and celery. Chop the rest of the garlic and chuck it in. Strip the leaves from the remaining thyme, chuck them in, then cook until the vegetables are soft but not browned.

Meanwhile, put the lentils in a saucepan, cover with cold water, bring to the boil, then drain them immediately and rinse them in hot water. Add them to the vegetables, then add the pork and enough of the reserved broth to cover the meat. Cover the pan and simmer very gently for 30–40 minutes, or until the lentils and pork are tender.

Cut the pork into thick slices. Reduce the lentils a little over a high heat, if needed, then stir in the mustard and parsley, check the seasoning and spoon into a serving dish. Arrange the pork on top, and eat with crusty bread and more mustard.

{ **SERVES 6** }

6 cloves garlic
1.3–1.8 kb/3–4 lb slab of pork belly, fairly lean, bones in
copious coarse sea salt (350–500 g/12–18 oz)
bunch of thyme
3 bay leaves
12 black peppercorns
3 tablespoons goose fat or olive oil
3 onions, roughly chopped
3 carrots, peeled and roughly chopped
2 celery stalks, roughly chopped
400 g/14 oz Puy lentils
3 tablespoons smooth Dijon mustard, plus extra to serve
big bunch of parsley, finely chopped
crusty bread, to serve

Penne all'amatriciana

{ SERVES 4 }

3 tablespoons olive oil

600 g/1 lb 5 oz smoked pancetta, cut into strips about 5 mm/¼ inch thick and 4 cm/1½ inches long

4 red onions, finely chopped

big pinch of dried peperoncino or dried chilli flakes or 2–5 dried bird's-eye chillies, finely chopped

3 large sprigs of rosemary, stripped and finely chopped

250 ml/9 fl oz red wine

4 x 400 g/14 oz cans chopped tomatoes

sea salt and freshly ground black pepper

125 g/4½ oz Parmesan, grated, plus extra to serve

500 g/1 lb 2 oz dried penne

This is one of the first dishes I cooked regularly after leaving university, and was a stalwart when having girls over for dinner. It took a couple of hours, smelt wondrous and tasted divine. It also gave time for a few glasses of wine. This was all about seduction via the stomach.

Heat the oil in a large heavy-bottomed saucepan over a medium–high heat and fry the pancetta until crisp. Reduce the heat to medium, add the onions and cook for about 10 minutes, until soft. Add the chilli and rosemary and cook for 2 minutes.

Chuck in the wine and increase the heat to burn off the alcohol; stir to deglaze the pan. Add the tomatoes and check the seasoning.

Turn down the heat to very low and cook, lid off, at a very slow blip for 2½–3 hours, until the sauce is thick and dry. Stir more frequently towards the end of cooking as the sauce thickens. Add grated Parmesan.

Cook the penne according to the packet instructions. Drain and mix with the sauce (don't overwhelm with sauce; the pasta should have equal billing) and serve immediately. Grate over some more Parmesan if you like.

Greek-style roast lamb with macaroni

{ SERVES 4 }

1 kg/2 lb 2 oz lamb shoulder, cut into 4, with the bone left in (ask your butcher to chop the lamb)
1 small lemon, halved
sea salt and freshly ground black pepper
1 tablespoon plain flour, seasoned
2 tablespoons olive oil
1 kg/2 lb 2 oz fresh or canned tomatoes, roughly chopped
250 ml/9 fl oz dry white wine
2 tablespoons tomato purée
3 cloves
1 cinnamon stick, broken

For the macaroni
900 ml/1½ pints full-fat milk
150 g/5½ oz butter, plus extra for greasing
75 g/2½ oz plain flour
1 egg yolk
450 g/1 lb long Greek macaroni
3 egg whites
125 g/4½ oz *kefalotyri* or pecorino cheese, grated
50 g/1¾ oz breadcrumbs, toasted

The Greeks are masters of lamb. And one of my favourite lunches of the year is at Greek Easter. I go to my friend Noli's house (well, his parents', anyway), and they roast a whole lamb on the spit as well as making an epic tripe soup. This recipe is more practical than the first, and less polarising than the second. It has a subtle spicing and real depth. If you can't find long Greek macaroni, look for the Italian equivalent. Or even normal macaroni if desperate, although the aesthetic effect is somewhat lost.

Preheat the oven to 150°C/300°F/Gas 2. Rub the lamb with the lemon, squeezing over the juice and reserving the rinds, and season. Cover and put in the fridge to marinate for 15–20 minutes. Dice the lemon rinds and set aside. Dust the lamb with seasoned flour. Heat the olive oil in a heavy roasting tin over a medium–high heat, add the lamb and brown it all over. Add the tomatoes and cook until bubbling.

Mix the wine with the tomato purée and add to the lamb, followed by the cloves, cinnamon and diced lemon rind. Pour in enough water (about 150 ml/5 fl oz) to cover the meat. Loosely cover the pan with foil and bake in the oven for 2½–3 hours, until the meat is falling off the bone.

After 1½–2 hours cooking, make the sauce for the macaroni. Warm the milk in a saucepan. In a separate saucepan, melt 75 g/2½ oz butter over a low heat until foaming. Add the flour a little at a time, whisking, until smooth. Remove from the heat.

{ CONTINUES OVERLEAF }

Slowly add the warm milk, whisking continuously to prevent lumps forming. Place the sauce back over a low heat and cook for 3–4 minutes, stirring often, until it has thickened to the consistency of cream.

Remove the sauce from the heat and season. Lightly whisk the egg yolk and beat it into the sauce. Set aside.

Lightly butter a large, shallow baking dish. Bring a large pan of salted water to the boil and cook the macaroni for half the time recommended on the packet. Drain and lay it out on a tray.

Melt the remaining butter in a small saucepan. In a bowl, whisk the egg whites until fluffy. Stir in half the melted butter, then pour this mixture over the macaroni, turning to coat evenly.

Put a thin layer of sauce in the bottom of the prepared baking dish. Sprinkle with a little cheese, then add a layer of macaroni. Sprinkle with more cheese, and a little more sauce and another layer of macaroni. Repeat until all the macaroni and sauce have been used. Sprinkle over the remaining cheese, then sprinkle over the breadcrumbs and top with the rest of the melted butter.

Thirty minutes before the lamb is ready, turn up the oven to 200°C/400°F/Gas 6. Remove the foil from the lamb to brown the meat and reduce the juices in the pan to a rich, sticky sauce. Bake the macaroni on the top shelf of the oven for 30 minutes, or until golden brown and crisp on top. Serve alongside the lamb.

Shoulder of lamb with pommes boulangère

{ SERVES 4 }

4 large onions, about 600 g/1 lb 5 oz, thinly sliced
big bunch of thyme
sea salt and freshly ground black pepper
1.25 kg/2 lb 12 oz Maris Piper potatoes, sliced into 1 cm/½ inch thick rounds
1 whole shoulder of lamb, about 1.5–2 kg/3½–4 ½ lb, excess fat removed
1 tablespoon Gentleman's Relish
1 head garlic, separated into cloves, peeled
10–12 small sprigs of rosemary
1.2 litres/2 pints hot chicken stock (cubes OK, but home-made better)

This really does require the minimum of preparation, but dear God, it's good. The lamb sits atop a tray of potatoes wallowing in stock, mixed with onion and a little thyme. As the meat cooks, slow and low, the juices infuse into the broth. You'll end up with lamb that disintegrates very pleasingly. And some of the most seductive potatoes you'll ever meet. You want to slice the potatoes about 1 cm/½ inch thick, so they keep some shape at the end. A mandolin does make things a lot easier, but a knife will do.

As for the Gentleman's Relish, don't panic. Some people hate the stuff, others worship it. The Victorians and Edwardians couldn't get enough anchovy butter and essence. Anchovies and lamb are natural bedfellows and, once the heat hits the relish, it loses any fishy aggression (like South-East Asian fish sauce) and adds a wonderful umami-infused extra level of flavour.

Preheat the oven to 150°C/300°F/Gas 2.

Take a large Le Creuset-type rectangular dish (Pyrex is fine, too) and fill with a layer of onions, then sprinkle with thyme, salt and pepper. Then add a layer of potatoes, making sure they cover the onions. Repeat the layers of onions, thyme, seasoning and potatoes until everything is used up, ending up with a layer of potatoes.

Make 10–12 slits in the lamb. Shove a smear of Gentleman's Relish, a clove of garlic and a small sprig of rosemary into each slit, until all the holes are filled and the shoulder resembles a Tim Burton hedgehog. Season.

Pour the stock over the potatoes and onions, until just covered. Put the shoulder of lamb on top and bake, uncovered, in the oven for 4 hours, or until cooked.

Rabbit & cider casserole

Wild rabbits. Millions of the buggers, infesting the countryside, yet the vast majority of us shy away, seeing them as a 'difficult' meat alongside other game. But they have a mild flavour and excellent texture, though they do tend towards dryness. Wild are the best and any decent butcher should be able to get hold of them. He'll also joint them for you. They're cheap, too. Farmed rabbits are available but have all the depth of a baking sheet. This is a dish with a proper West Country burr, to be accompanied by a dry cider, preferably from Burrow Hill in Somerset.

Season 4 tablespoons flour generously, then roll the rabbit pieces in it, shaking off any excess. Heat the oil in a heavy-bottomed casserole over a medium–high heat and fry the rabbit for 5 minutes, turning once or twice, until golden brown. Remove from the pan and drain on kitchen paper.

Add the butter to the pan, then tip in the onion. Reduce the heat to medium and fry the onion for 10 minutes, until softened and golden. Stir in the remaining 3 tablespoons flour then add the bay leaf and thyme. Gradually pour in the cider and chicken stock, stirring continuously. Increase the heat to high and bring to the boil, stirring.

Return the rabbit to the casserole, taste and season. Cover, then reduce the heat to low and simmer for about 2 hours, or until the meat is tender and almost falling off the bone. (Alternatively, transfer the casserole to an oven preheated to 150°C/300°F/Gas 2 for 2 hours.)

Using a slotted spoon, remove the rabbit from the casserole and set aside on a warm plate. Pour the cream into the casserole and simmer gently for a few minutes, until slightly thicker. Return the rabbit to the casserole, along with any juices, then adjust the seasoning and sprinkle over the parsley. Serve with the cabbage and mashed potatoes.

{ SERVES 4 }

7 tablespoons plain flour

sea salt and freshly ground black pepper

2 rabbits (wild, if possible), jointed

2 tablespoons olive oil

25 g/1 oz butter

1 onion, roughly chopped

1 bay leaf

2 sprigs thyme

400 ml/14 fl oz good dry cider

500 ml/18 fl oz chicken stock

3 tablespoons double cream

small handful curly parsley, roughly chopped

steamed cabbage with crisp cooked bacon and mashed potatoes, to serve

{ From far-flung shores }

These are recipes gleaned from ten years of travelling in total thrall to my gut. My tastes are resolutely low. Give me decent street food over the most elaborate of Michelin-starred confections. It's no coincidence that two of my favourite cuisines in the world, Mexican and Thai, have the most thriving pavement tucker you'll find anywhere. Many of the recipes in this chapter are adapted street-food dishes, and while you'll never be able to replicate sitting outside a Mexico City *taquería* munching on *tacos al pastor*, or perching on a wobbly plastic stool in Bangkok while wolfing down green papaya salad, I hope they give a decent approximation.

Don't be put off by the long lists of strange ingredients, or the sometimes seemingly endless preparation needed. Nothing is overly difficult or elaborate, and nothing requires any specific skill beyond handling a knife or pounding a pestle and mortar. The cooking is the easiest bit of all. Once the prep is in place, the rest is a cinch. And in our bold new digital age, even the most obscure of shrimp pastes and Central American herbs are but a click away.

{ Chillies }

You may have noticed that chillies play a starring role in many of my recipes. I love these pungent pods in their every form, bow down to their versatile brilliance, worship at the altar of capsaicin, the irritant alkaloid that gives chillies their heat.

It all started with my first taste of a Madras curry. Before long, I was after bigger kicks, getting mired deeper and deeper into a dangerous and pulse-quickening world. Vindaloo came next, and I rarely travelled without a bottle of Tabasco close to hand. Thai soups and salads followed, the sort that bead the forehead in sweat and render any conversation impossible. From there, it was a slippery slope to sinister-sounding hot sauces – Blair's Ultra Death, Da' Bomb, Dave's Insanity. And before I knew it, I was subscribing to *Chile Pepper Magazine*, growing my own Scotch bonnets and scouring the streets late at night, desperate for a hit of something fierce and red.

There's no doubt that chillies are addictive. Sure, there's pain, often wave after wave of it, enough to bring you to your knees. Once, a few years back, I went to the National Fiery Foods Show in Albuquerque, New Mexico. Emboldened by a few beers, I decided to try one particular sauce that came in at two million on the Scoville scale (this measures chilli heat – Tabasco sits around 5,000). So this extract sauce (meaning it uses chemically extracted capsaicin, the same thing you'd find in pepper spray), called something like Exquisite Agony, was fierce. I tasted only the tiniest amount, enough to cover the head of a pin. But dear God, did it hurt. So much so that I hit the ground, bent double, my tongue a useless, throbbing mass of dead flesh, my throat aflame, my whole nervous system in revolt. Even thinking pained me. Then came the endorphins, released to fight the pain, charging in like valiant troopers to quash the infidel horde. And slowly, very slowly, I came back to life. What followed was that soft, toasty afterburn, where colours seemed sharper, sounds amplified and smells became that much more vivid. This experience, to a greater or lesser extent, has been repeated all over the world, from Thai markets to Mexican cantinas. My wife just shakes her head, while friends are so used to my grunting and sweating that they just carry on eating, regardless.

But chillies are not all about heat. They're about flavour, too. That's why I love the food of Mexico, India and Thailand. The fresh habaneros and bird's-eye chillies are fiercely hot, but they have their own character too. And there's a world of difference between the green kick of a jalapeño and the mild appeal of a banana chilli. When dried, many chillies become more complex and rich – the serious, smoky heft of the chipotle (a smoked dried

'Before I knew it, I was subscribing to Chile Pepper Magazine, growing my own Scotch Bonnets and scouring the streets late at night, desperate for a hit of something fierce and red.'

jalapeño), the sharp charm of the ancho, the chocolate warmth of the mulato. Depending on your tastes, you can adjust the level of heat in the recipes to your liking.

And despite my love for the chilli, I'm not so obsessed that I would use it out of context. I don't douse Yorkshire puddings with Caribbean hot sauce, nor do I spike my ragù alla Bolognese with Hungarian hot wax. That said, a week without heat and my body starts craving. The chilli is unquestionably the greatest of all fruits, the ingredient I love above all other. A life spent without it would be very dull indeed.

Top row from left: jalapeño and Thai bird's-eye chillies
Second row from left: cayenne, habaneros, chipotle meco, chipotle morita
Bottom row from left: ancho, Thai dried red chillies and chipotle morita

{ Thai food }

The best lunches often occur in the most incongruous of places. It was just after noon, deep in the *khlongs* (canals) of Bangkok. The sun beat down and all was languid, save the occasional put-put of riverboats selling noodles, chillies and herbs in every hue of green.

We were with David Thompson, one of the world's great Thai chefs and the author of *Thai Food* (Pavilion 2002), the finest work on this cuisine in the English language. And we were hungry. Suddenly, without warning, he tells the boat driver to stop. We pull up at a makeshift pontoon, where a noodle seller is bent over bubbling pots. You choose your noodles and whatever you want on top – fish balls, chicken or prawns – then everything is covered with a rich pork broth. You add fish sauce, or fresh chilli, or dried chilli powder to taste ('Every dish in Thailand is personalised at the table,' says David, 'a touch of sugar, a handful of chillies, whatever.') and dig in.

The lunch was simplicity itself, but every element was divine – the broth clean, fresh and fragrant, and the noodles made that morning, still slightly chewy. A squeeze of lime for a citrus kick, the chillies' fierce, floral heat. I just kept eating, bowl after bowl. This was food as it should be, glorious, cheap and unpretentious. Sweating with joy and chilli heat, I ask David how many times he'd been here before. Surely this place was famous? He shook his head. 'Never been here before. But this is Thailand. They're obsessed with food. If it wasn't any good, it would be gone in days.'

The next few days were spent in a wanton orgy of eating. Oyster omelettes, frazzled at the bottom, gooey on top. Fish-gut curries, fierce and sinister; slightly fermented pork sausages, plump and tart, green papaya salads so hot that time seemed to slow down and you entered a capsaicin-fuelled nether world of pain and pleasure.

'Food is the only democratic institution in Thailand,' David told us en route to yet another feast. 'It's a unifying force. Thai food from region to region is as distinct as that of Italy or France. They don't much care about politics. The only time there are real riots is when the rice is too expensive. When they're not eating, they're thinking about what they're going to eat, or working out where they'll eat. When in bed, they'll dream about it. Good food is not just a luxury for the rich. Thai people really do eat to live and live to eat.'

Balance is everything: of the hot, sweet, salty and sour. Some dishes will just use two of these elements, while others will use three or four. But Thai cooking is all about the juggling of ingredients and disparate, often potent flavours to create one harmonious whole.

In Bangkok and the central plains region, with its historic wealth and countless outside influences, dishes can be complex. The many rivers provide abundant prawns, catfish and crabs, and hot and salty is probably the dominant taste. This is the home of sour orange curries and fiery *tom yam gung* (hot-and-sour prawn soup). The street food has a strong Chinese influence.

In the north, plain rice becomes sticky, coconuts are rare, and shrimp paste nowhere near as important to cooking as it is in the central plains – although hot and salty rules here, too. Pork is king; game and various reptiles are eaten. *Kao soi*, a curried noodle dish with roots in China, is a speciality of Chiang Mai. And the Chiang Mai sausage, slightly sour, is another favourite.

The northeast, or Isarn region, was traditionally isolated, with many different ethnic groups. The region is poor and predominantly rural, the food very hot. Less food to dress the rice means more intensity of flavour, heat and pungency, is needed. Various versions of *larp*, a salad of minced meat or fish, are popular, as they are in neighbouring Laos. There's also all manner of insects (ant-egg soup is pretty good), snakes and jungle cats. People here have little time for Western squeamishness, rather eating whatever they can to survive. Thailand's south has vivid, almost gaudy, food, and dried bird's-eye chillies reign supreme. There's lots of coconut, fruit in the curries and, of course, seafood.

In Britain, Thai food is pretty dire. Everything seems over-sweet, deep-fried and emasculated, as if all the interesting parts – the shrimp paste with its tang of the sewer, the chilli heat, the elegance and balance of flavours – are too much for our tender palates. Thompson's view is that the Thai people are so hospitable that they give us what they think we want, rather than cooking as they do at home. And he's right. Armed with this knowledge, I marched into my local Thai and demanded, politely, the food they were eating. At first, they ignored the *farang* (foreigner) and smiled sweetly. But I persisted. And suddenly they relented, and the food came alive. I was eating proper Thai food, minutes away from Bayswater tube.

The recipes here are all classics, some of it street food (which is mainly Chinese in origin), some home cooking. All, though, make the senses sing. If you don't like the chillies, cut the quantity down. The dried ones have a slow-burning heat, while the fresh scuds are lethal but utterly addictive. As ever, fiddle until you find what you like. They may not all be entirely authentic. But compared to the usual lifeless pap served up in the name of Thai food, they're a whole new world of edible delight.

Thai beef salad

This is a classic of Thai cookery; incredibly simple to make but it does take a little preparation for the chilli and rice powders. I tend to make them both in big batches and store them in an airtight box or bottle. With these to hand, the dish can be made in moments. It mixes the sour with the hot, and the rice powder gives a wonderful golden crunch.

Mix the shallots with the herbs and divide between 2 plates.

Rub the steak with a little oil and season. Preheat a griddle pan to hot and cook the steak for 2 minutes on each side, then leave to rest for 2 minutes. Slice it thinly and lay the slices on top of the herbs and shallots.

To make the dressing, mix together the fish sauce, lime juice and roasted chilli powder. Pour over the salad, then sprinkle with the roasted rice powder.

{ **Roasted chilli powder** } Heat a small heavy-based pan to smoking hot and dry-fry 6 dried long Thai chillies for about 1 minute – open the windows as the fumes could bring down an elephant. Remove from the heat, leave to cool and grind the chillies to a powder using a pestle and mortar.

{ **Roasted rice powder** } Heat a small heavy-based pan over a medium–low heat and dry-fry uncooked white sticky rice for 2–3 minutes, until the rice starts to toast and give off a wonderful burnished biscuity smell. Crush using a pestle and mortar.

{ SERVES 2 }

6 Thai shallots, thinly sliced
good handful each of mint, coriander and holy basil leaves
500 g/1 lb 2 oz thick-cut sirloin steak
vegetable oil
sea salt and freshly ground black pepper

For the dressing
3 tablespoons fish sauce
5 tablespoons lime juice
2 big pinches of roasted chilli powder (see method)
1 tablespoon roasted rice powder (see method)

From far-flung shores

Stir-fried beef with cumin

{ SERVES 2 }

300 g/10½ oz trimmed
   beef rump
2 tablespoons fish sauce
big pinch of roasted chilli
   powder (see page 199)
8 dried red chillies, toasted
3 tablespoons groundnut oil
1½ heaped tablespoons cumin
   and chilli paste (see below)
1 teaspoon palm or caster sugar
2 teaspoons rice wine vinegar
4 teaspoons tamarind water
   (see page 207)
1 red onion, cut into wedges
bunch of coriander,
   roughly chopped
steamed rice, to serve

For the cumin and chilli paste
2 teaspoons cumin seeds
6 dried red Thai chillies,
   deseeded and soaked in
   warm water for 30 minutes,
   then drained
½ teaspoon sea salt
5 Thai shallots, finely chopped
6 cloves garlic, finely chopped

I've hugely adapted this recipe from David Thompson and I'm sure he – and Matthew Albert, his equally talented head chef at Nahm in London – would be appalled. Like all Thai food, there's a bit of preparation involved. But the end result is quick to cook and well worth the effort.

First, make the cumin and chilli paste. Heat a small pan over low–medium heat, add the cumin seeds and dry-fry until fragrant. Leave to cool, then grind using a pestle and mortar or electric spice grinder. Pound the chillies and salt together using a pestle and mortar, then add the shallots, garlic and 1 teaspoon of the freshly ground cumin (reserve the rest for the beef); grind to a paste. This will make about 4 tablespoons; keep whatever you don't use in the fridge for up to 3 days.

Cut the beef into thin slices across the grain. Mix the fish sauce, roasted chilli powder and remaining ground cumin in a bowl, add the whole dried toasted chillies and the beef. Coat the beef in the marinade, cover and leave to marinate in the fridge for 30 minutes.

Heat the oil in a wok until smoking, then take the beef and whole chillies out of the marinade and fry until the beef colours, 1–2 minutes. Add 1½ heaped tablespoons of the cumin and chilli paste, breaking it up and stirring until it becomes fragrant. Then add the sugar, vinegar and tamarind water and simmer for 1 minute. Taste. It should be hot, salty and rich with cumin. A little sticky, too.

Remove from the heat and stir through the red onion quarters and coriander. Serve with steamed rice.

Minced beef with chillies & basil

A Thai street-food staple, although a relatively recent one. Of course, you'll never be able to replicate the smoky tinge that comes from a veteran, battle-scarred street wok. But this has it all – slightly frazzled beef, oozing fried egg, the ubiquitous chilli and the clovey, slightly tongue-numbing holy basil. Get the best beef you can afford, preferably coarsely minced sirloin.

Finely chop the garlic with a pinch of salt and the chillies.

Add half the oil to a wok or frying pan and heat until smoking. Fry the eggs, then set aside and keep warm.

To make the dipping sauce, mix the fish sauce, garlic and chillies. Set aside. Just before serving, add the lime juice and coriander.

Add the remaining oil to the wok or pan, heat until smoking, then fry the garlic and chilli mixture for a few moments. Add the beef and cook for 1 minute, then add the fish sauce and sugar.

Add the stock and simmer for a few seconds, then stir in the basil. Divide between 2 bowls and serve with a fried egg on top. Serve with steamed white rice and the dipping sauce.

{ SERVES 2 }

3 cloves garlic, peeled
salt
3–10 bird's-eye chillies
3 tablespoons groundnut oil
2 eggs
300 g/10½ oz minced beef
1 tablespoon fish sauce
large pinch of granulated sugar
1 tablespoon chicken stock
2 large handfuls holy basil leaves
steamed Thai fragrant rice,
   to serve

For the dipping sauce
50 ml/2 fl oz fish sauce
1 clove garlic, finely sliced
3–10 bird's-eye chillies,
   finely chopped
2 tablespoons lime juice
pinch of finely chopped
   fresh coriander

From far-flung shores

Spicy pork balls

{ SERVES 4 }

2 chillies, preferably Thai bird's-eye, finely sliced
½ lemongrass stalk
small handful of coriander, ideally with roots, finely chopped
handful of mint, finely chopped
handful of Thai basil, finely chopped
good pinch of freshly ground black pepper
400 g/14 oz free-range minced pork
2 tablespoons groundnut oil
2 iceberg lettuces, leaves separated, to serve

For the dipping sauce

4 bird's-eye chillies, finely chopped
1 clove garlic, thinly sliced
pinch of caster sugar
2 tablespoons lime juice
1 tablespoon fish sauce

This Thai dish is good for snack or starter. It's hard to find minced free-range pork from the butcher, but do search it out. It's far preferable to the insipid supermarket stuff. The herbs, as ever, lift the dish from the everyday to the exquisite, while the iceberg lettuce, much maligned, adds cool crunch.

Crush the chillies, lemongrass, herbs and black pepper in a pestle and mortar or a blender. Mix well with the minced pork.

Shape the mixture into about 20 small balls (wet your hands so the mixture doesn't stick).

Heat the oil in a frying pan over a medium heat and fry the balls all over for 8–10 minutes, until cooked inside. Cut one in half; it should be evenly coloured with no traces of pink – if not, cook for a little longer. Drain on kitchen paper.

To make the dipping sauce, combine the chillies, garlic, sugar, lime juice and fish sauce in a small bowl.

Pile the pork balls on a plate and serve with the lettuce leaves and dipping sauce.

Larp gai (Laotian chicken salad)

It took mere minutes to fall in love with Laos, that landlocked South-East Asian country still scarred by the Vietnam War. Overshadowed by its immediate neighbours, China and Burma to the north, Vietnam to the east, Cambodia to the south and Thailand to the west, it's one of the world's few remaining Communist states. Not that this bothers the residents, who are some of the most open and hospitable people I've ever met. Vientiane has to be the most laid-back capital in the world. Even the traffic lights change at languorous pace. And Luang Phrabang, the ancient royal capital, is better still, dreamily tranquil and endlessly beautiful, studded with temples and cut through by the mighty Mekong River.

It's a poor country, with many living way below the poverty line. In rural areas you'll find markets selling jungle cats and frogs, snakes, insects, even dried rats. The water beetles, great fat beasts, were rather good, with a taste of pear drops. And the deep-fried bee pupae were far superior to the dullard peanut as a bar snack. But it's *larp* (or *larb*) I ate the most: pretty much the national dish, it's a riot of tastes and textures. Traditionally made with minced water buffalo meat; rather hard to come by in the local Tesco – you can use minced pork, or, as in this recipe, chicken instead.

{ **SERVES 2** }

150 ml/5 fl oz chicken stock
big pinch of sugar (palm if possible but caster is fine)
350 g/12 oz chicken breast, minced by hand
5 tablespoons lime juice
2 tablespoons fish sauce
4–5 bird's-eye chillies, chopped
2 large pinches of roasted chilli powder (see page 201)
5 Thai shallots, thinly sliced
handful of mint, coarsely chopped
handful of coriander, finely chopped
2 large pinches of roasted fine rice powder (see page 201)

Combine the stock and sugar in a saucepan and bring to a simmer. Add the chicken and simmer gently for 5–10 minutes, or until cooked through.

Remove from the heat and add the lime juice, fish sauce, chillies, chilli powder, shallots and herbs.

Sprinkle with the roasted rice powder and serve.

From far-flung shores

Chicken, lime & lemongrass soup

{ **SERVES 2** }

2 litres/3½ pints fresh chicken stock (*see* page 38), boiled to reduce to 1 litre/1¾ pints
2 lemongrass stalks, bruised
4 slices of galangal, each about the size of a £1 coin
9 Thai shallots, peeled
2 chicken breasts (the best you can afford)
6 tablespoons lime juice
3–4 tablespoons fish sauce
big pinch of finely chopped bird's-eye chillies
1 tablespoon finely chopped lemongrass
handful of roughly chopped coriander, to garnish

A deeply soothing, medicinal broth. It's incredibly easy to make, although you do need good stock. You get waves of lime, lemongrass and galangal that all work in heavenly harmony. A dish we eat pretty much every week. It builds layer upon layer of flavour. Marinating the cooked chicken in the fish sauce and lime base gives an extra level of zing.

Put the stock in a large pan, bring to a simmer and add the lemongrass stalks, galangal and 3 whole shallots. Simmer for 10 minutes.

Add the chicken breasts, cover and simmer for a further 10–12 minutes, or until they are cooked through. Turn off the heat, remove the chicken, leave to cool and then shred. Strain the stock, discarding the aromatics.

Slice the remaining 6 shallots. Divide the shredded chicken between 2 bowls and add 3 tablespoons of lime juice and 1½–2 tablespoons of fish sauce to each. Add the shallots, chillies and lemongrass and leave for 20 minutes.

Reheat the stock until boiling, pour over the chicken and mix. Finish with a handful of chopped coriander.

Green papaya salad

{ SERVES 2 OR 4 AS A SIDE DISH }

3 cloves garlic, peeled
sea salt
1 heaped teaspoon roasted peanuts, crushed
2 tablespoons dried prawns (optional)
4 cherry tomatoes, quartered
5 green beans, sliced into 1 cm/½ inch lengths
5 bird's-eye chillies
225 g/8 oz green papaya, shredded
2 tablespoons palm or caster sugar
1 tablespoon lime juice
1 tablespoon tamarind water (see below)
2 tablespoons fish sauce
steamed Thai rice, to serve
Chinese cabbage, quartered, to serve

I'll never forget my first bite. I was 18, greener than a young papaya, and in Bangkok for the first time. Having just spent 6 months in the Indian wilderness, arriving in the garish, neon-soaked Thai capital was like that moment where Dorothy arrives in Oz, and the screen changes from monochrome to glorious Technicolor. Anyway, the first street-food vendor I found (or plucked up the courage to approach) was selling a sort of greeny-white salad in a bag. I did a lot of pointing and nodding and was asked, 'How hot?' Chest puffed up, I answered, 'Thai hot. Like you.' He smiled, but did as I asked. The first bite was astonishing. The crunch of green papaya, the saline chew of dried shrimps, a tang of lime, and a mouth-puckering hit of tamarind. Then the chillies took hold, coming in wave after wave, increasing in ferocity until even my brain throbbed in pain. I had to sit down, head in hand, hyperventilating. The vendors howled with laughter. Once the pain had subsided, though, I wanted more.

Pound the garlic with a pinch of salt in a pestle and mortar. Add the peanuts and dried prawns and continue pounding to a coarse paste. Add the tomatoes and beans, pounding lightly. Add the chillies. The more you pound them, the more oils disperse and the hotter it gets. So beware.

Put the shredded papaya in a large bowl, add the chilli mixture and continue to bruise and mix with the pestle. Season with the sugar, lime, tamarind water and fish sauce. Serve with rice and Chinese cabbage.

{ **Tamarind water** } If you can get fresh tamarind, pull off a few sticky buds and put them in warm water for 5 minutes. Mulch between your fingertips, then push through a sieve. Alternatively, soak 1 teaspoon dried tamarind in 2 tablespoons boiling water for 5 minutes, then strain through a fine sieve.

Shrimp broth

When I first tried this, deep in Soho on a dull Sunday afternoon, I was rendered speechless. It had such intensity, and depth, from relatively few basic ingredients. To re-create it, I used dried shrimps from a Chinese supermarket and they worked just fine. Guajillo chillies are dried chillies with a mild flavour: you can get them from the Cool Chile Co (**www.coolchile.co.uk**), or try using about 4–6 dried bird's-eye chillies. Totally different flavour, but works well.

Put the shrimps in a saucepan, add 2 litres/3½ pints water, bring to the boil, then simmer for 15 minutes.

Meanwhile, toast the chillies in a dry frying pan until fragrant, then soak them in boiling water for 20 minutes, until soft.

Heat the vegetable oil in a saucepan. Add the onions and soften over a medium heat for 5 minutes. Add the celery, carrots, parsley sprigs and avocado leaves, if using. Cook for 15 minutes. Add the potatoes for the last 4 minutes.

When the shrimp cooking time is up, remove them from the broth with a slotted spoon and set aside. Strain the broth into a jug. Liquidise the soaked chillies with a tablespoon of the shrimps.

Return the broth to the pan, add the softened vegetables, stir in the shrimps and shrimp-chilli paste and simmer for a further 10 minutes. Serve with quartered limes.

{ SERVES 8 }

200 g/7 oz dried shrimps

3 guajillo chillies, deseeded and opened out

1 tablespoon vegetable oil

2 white onions, finely chopped

1 small celery stalk, finely chopped

5 carrots, cut into cubed

3 sprigs parsley

3 avocado leaves (optional)

4 waxy potatoes, peeled and cut into cubes

6 limes, quartered

From far-flung shores

{ Mexican food }

Why is it that Mexican food has such a wretched reputation in the UK? After all, this is a Titan among cuisines, astonishingly varied and endlessly exciting. From the lip-tingling ceviches of *Baja California* to *mole negro* in Oaxaca, Jaliscan whole grilled fish, naked save a squeeze of lime, to pig heaven with Yucatán *cochinita pibil* – not forgetting *tacos al pastor* in Mexico City, among a thousand other culinary delights – this vast country has it all.

The Mexicans are masters of the chilli, using it fresh and dried for heat and flavour. Some, such as the fresh *poblano* and dried *pasilla*, are mild and rich. Others, like the fruit-scented habanero, can take off the top of your head.

At the heart of everything is corn, which we know as maize. The smell of cooking *masa* dough (maize slaked with calcium hydroxide or lime) is the scent of Mexico. Tacos, the soft corn tortillas, are ubiquitous, but there are myriad ways with this most essential of ingredients: *gordas* (griddled pockets), *sopes* (small fried discs), *chalupas*, *memelas*, *picadas*, *quesadillas*, *panuchos*. The Mexicans are food fanatics, stopping at any opportunity for a crisp *flauta*, stuffed with pork, or a shrimp taco, or *quesadilla*. This is a culture built around eating.

So how come the British see Mexican food as greasy, tasteless and turgid, with a tendency to squat in the belly like a cheese-coated shot put? 'Tex-Mex', that's why, a nauseating blend of bad mariachi music, second-rate Tequila and sizzling platters of, well, I'm not sure what.

Anyone brave enough to venture into their local 'Break For the Border', 'Sombreros and Slammers' or 'Greedy Gonzales' takes their digestive well-being into very dangerous territory. The guacamole is slopped from a vast catering pack, made months before and kept alive with a noxious cocktail of preservatives and colourings. The salsa comes straight from a jar, purse-lipped and mean, while the tortilla chips are little more than Doritos from the wrong side of the tracks. There are comedy cocktails in comedy glasses that stain the tongue in comedy colours and frozen margaritas sold by the foot. Along with bargain-basement chilli con carnes (not a Mexican dish, despite what these places might claim) with humorous names ('Ring of Fire', etc), overrun with beans and cheap mince. Everything comes buried in a slick of greasy, microwave-nuked cheese, even the puddings.

As you stagger out of the door, senses numbed and sweating despair, you vow never, ever, to eat 'Mexican' again. Of course, this is no more Mexican than Pizza Hut is Italian. But it matters not. The damage has been done. And this fine and mighty cuisine suffers another unwarranted blow, sullied and horribly debased.

It's not just the food that suffers from bad PR, but the whole country. Most people believe that Mexico is a war zone, with bullets sprayed willy-nilly and bodies piled waist high. There *is* a catastrophic narco war going on in the north, by the US border, and occasionally the violence spills out to Acapulco, or Mexico City. But Mexico is far more sinned against than sinning. And it's one of my favourite countries in the world.

I've been a dozen times, and always want to return. The smell of cooking corn, petrol fumes, grilling beef and roasting chillies. Bliss.

Some of these recipes come from my friend Alberto, a fantastic chef and native of Mexico City, with whom I've cooked on a couple of occasions. He is a master, I'm a mere apprentice. This is just a taste, but enough, I hope, to prove that Mexican food is many miles removed from that filth the British call 'Tex Mex'.

'The smell of cooking corn, petrol fumes, grilling beef and roasting chillies. Bliss.'

Mexican beef stew

{ SERVES 4 }

2 tablespoons olive oil
900 g/2 lb braising steak or shin, cut into 2.5 cm/1 inch cubes
2 onions, roughly chopped
2 cloves garlic, finely chopped
700 g/1 lb 9 oz jar of passata
2 tablespoons red wine vinegar
3–8 chipotles (soaked in warm water for 15 minutes, destemmed and finely chopped)
2 bay leaves
1 teaspoon dried Mexican oregano (European oregano would work, too)
sea salt

To serve
fresh corn tortillas
big bunch of coriander, finely chopped
300 ml/10 fl oz soured cream
handful of grated Cheddar

This has chipotle chillies – dried and smoked jalapeños – at its heart. They have a wonderful rich depth and really make the stew. You can get them and the Mexican oregano from the Cool Chile Co (**www.coolchile.co.uk**).

Preheat the oven to 150°C/300°F/Gas 2.

Heat the oil in a large flameproof casserole and brown the meat over a high heat, in batches. Scoop out of the pan and set aside. Reduce the heat to medium. Add the onions and garlic to the pan and soften for about 10 minutes.

Return the meat to the pan, add the passata, vinegar, chipotles, bay leaves, oregano and a big pinch of salt. Bring to the boil, then cover and cook in the oven for 3 hours, or until the meat is meltingly tender.

Serve with fresh tortillas, chopped coriander, soured cream and grated Cheddar.

Sambutes

{ MAKES 25–30 }

olive oil, for frying
1 onion, finely chopped
1 habanero or Scotch bonnet chilli, finely chopped
225 g/8 oz minced pork
several soft corn tortillas
50 g/1¾ oz plain flour, mixed with water to make a paste
300 ml/10 fl oz soured cream, to serve
salsa, to serve (see pages 226-7)

This is a take on *salbutes*, a classic dish from Mexico's Yucatán Peninsula. Deep-fried filled tortillas, stuffed with a spicy pork mix. This is habanero land – big fruit, mega kick.

Heat a little olive oil in a large, heavy-based frying pan and soften the onion and chilli over a medium–high heat. Add the pork and cook for 4–5 minutes, stirring frequently, until lightly browned.

Using a 5-cm/2-inch cookie cutter cut 50–60 small circles from the tortillas.

Put 1 heaped teaspoon of the pork mixture on to a tortilla circle, then top with another tortilla circle, using flour paste to seal the edges and pinching them together.

Heat 5 cm/2 inches of oil in a wide, heavy-based pan over medium–high heat and fry the *sambutes* in batches for 2–3 minutes, turning once, until golden brown and cooked through. Drain on kitchen paper.

Serve the hot *sambutes* with the soured cream and salsa if you like.

Cochinita pibil

{ SERVES 8 }

2 tablespoons cumin seeds
1 tablespoon juniper berries
10 cloves
85 g/3 oz *recado de achiote* paste (www.coolchile.co.uk)
500 ml/18 fl oz Seville orange juice (or, if out of season, 400 ml/14 fl oz freshly squeezed orange juice and 100 ml/3½ fl oz lemon juice)
sea salt
1 large pork shoulder, boned, cut into large cubes
1 packet of banana leaves (www.theasiancookshop.co.uk) (optional)
cooked tortillas, to serve
salsa, to serve (see pages 226–7)

A classic dish from the Yucatán region of Mexico, transforming a shoulder of pork into meltingly tender strands of piggy bliss. It's traditionally cooked in the *pib*, a pit lined with hot stones. The meat is wrapped in banana leaves, dropped onto the searing stones, then covered with wet sacking, followed by more hot rocks and embers, then a final topping of earth to fill the pit. This could prove impractical in the average British kitchen, so a slow oven is fine. *Achiote* paste (made from the small red seeds of the annatto tree) gives the all-important red colour and a good depth of flavour. Seville orange juice is best for the marinade, but it has only a short winter season. Fresh orange juice (not that horrible concentrated stuff) mixed with a little lemon is a good substitute.

Grind the cumin, juniper berries and cloves in a coffee grinder. Blend the spice mix, *achiote* paste and orange juice in a food processor. Season with salt to taste.

Marinate the cubes of pork shoulder in the spiced orange juice, covered, in the fridge for at least 12 hours.

Preheat the oven to 170°C/325°F/Gas 3.

Wash the banana leaves, if using, and quickly pass them over a burner to soften them or blanch them in a pan of boiling water. Line a roasting tin with the banana leaves, making sure that you'll be able to fold them over the pork once you place it in the tin. (If you can't get banana leaves, cook the pork in a covered casserole or a dish tightly covered with a double thickness of foil.) Add the pork and the marinade, cover with foil and cook in the oven for about 4-4½ hours, until tender. Ideally, leave it to cool, then put it in the fridge, covered, overnight. The next day, reheat thoroughly, adding a touch of oil.

An hour before you are going to eat the pork, make the chilli-pickled onion. Rinse the red onion in a strainer under cold water for a couple of minutes; leave to dry. Place the chilli in a bowl with the onion and cover with the cider vinegar. To serve, remove the onion from the vinegar.

When the pork is ready, use a fork to shred the meat, removing big chunks of fat. Serve with the juices, fresh tortillas and salsa.

For chilli-pickled red onions
1 red onion, thinly sliced
1 Scotch bonnet or habanero chilli, very thinly sliced
3 tablespoons cider vinegar

Guacamole

{ SERVES 8 }

5 ripe avocados
2 red onions, finely chopped
2 jalapeño or finger chillies,
    finely chopped
4 ripe tomatoes, skinned,
    deseeded and finely chopped
juice of 2 limes
sea salt and freshly ground
    black pepper

Real guacamole is a riot of textures, and manages to combine the creamy, sharp and spicy. The real thing is miles removed from that snot-green wallpaper paste that plays host to more chemicals than an ICI plant. The avocados must be ripe, so you can mash them with a fork – never use a food processor; I do like the odd chunk left in. Everyone's tastes are different, so feel free to increase onions and cut down on chillies and the rest.

Peel and destone the avocados and mash them roughly, using a large fork. Add the onions, chillies, tomatoes and lime juice. Season to taste and serve.

Mole verde

A *mole* is far more than mere sauce. 'The King of Mexican cuisine,' writes Patricia Quintana in *The Taste of Mexico* (1986). It's a true Mexican *mélange*, available in a thousand different variations. One of the richest, and certainly the most famous, is the *mole poblano* from Puebla: it melds anise, clove, cinnamon, black peppers and chillies with garlic, tomatillos, sesame seeds, ground almonds, peanuts and bitter chocolate. A complex and time-consuming dish, sure, but magnificent, too. This is a green version, thickened with toasted pumpkin seeds and made verdant with coriander, tomatillo and lettuce. It's rich and comforting, with a slight chilli kick.

Put 1.4 litres/2½ pints water in a saucepan, add the onion, bay leaf and a pinch of salt, and bring to the boil. Add the chicken pieces, ensuring they are fully immersed, skim off any scum, put a lid on and simmer gently for about 45 minutes, or until cooked through. Let the chicken cool in the broth, then remove it and set it aside. Strain the broth into a bowl and skim off the fat with kitchen paper.

To make the sauce, heat a frying pan over a medium heat for 5 minutes, then pour in the pumpkin seeds in a single layer. When the first seed pops, cook and stir for up to 5 minutes, until all have popped. Leave to cool. Grind in a food processor or spice grinder, then stir into 200 ml/7 fl oz of the chicken cooking broth.

{ CONTINUES OVERLEAF }

{ SERVES 4 }

1 onion, finely chopped
1 bay leaf
sea salt
1 x 1.8 kg/4 lb chicken (the best you can afford), cut in half, then half again
boiled rice, to serve

For the sauce

100 g/3½ oz pumpkin seeds
2 x 375 g cans tomatillos (www.coolchile.co.uk; or use homegrown green tomatoes or 2 x 400 g cans chopped tomatoes), drained
4 fresh jalapeño chillies (or from a jar in brine, drained), finely chopped
6 large romaine lettuce leaves
½ onion, roughly chopped
4 cloves garlic, roughly chopped
40 g/1½ oz coriander, plus extra to garnish
½ teaspoon cumin seeds
6 black peppercorns
2 cm/¾ inch piece of cinnamon stick
3–4 cloves
1 tablespoon lard or vegetable oil
sea salt

Put the tomatillos and chillies into a blender. Tear the lettuce leaves and add to the blender, along with the onion, garlic and coriander. Grind the cumin, peppercorns, cinnamon and cloves in a spice grinder or pestle and mortar, then add to the blender and blitz until smooth.

Heat the lard or oil in a large saucepan and, when hot, add the pumpkin seed mixture and cook, stirring, until it thickens and darkens – about 5 minutes. Add the tomatillo and spice blend and cook, stirring for a few more minutes, until darker still.

Add 400 ml/14 fl oz of the broth, reduce the heat to medium–low and simmer, partially covered, for about 30 minutes.

Shred the chicken, removing the skin, and add to the simmering sauce. Cook to heat through for 10 minutes. Serve with rice.

A trio of ceviches

Ceviche. One word guaranteed to pique the taste buds. Freshness of the fish is paramount, as you're serving it pretty much raw, save a light 'cooking' in acidic citrus juice. It should dance off the tongue, gloriously pert, refreshing and zingy.

Any country with a coastline in South and Central America will claim credit and each will proclaim theirs the best. In truth, the dish probably had Polynesian root, although anywhere with an abundant supply of fresh fish and acidic medium (citrus juice, vinegar) would have used this technique. In the Philippines I tried a dish called *kinilaw*, where raw fish is simply dipped in vinegar. Very good it was, too, and could even be the daddy of them all.

The fish needs no more than 30 minutes in the citrus juice – any longer and you obliterate the piscine sweetness with an acidic hammer. Chilli adds essential heat, red onions crunch and bite, tomatoes soft sweetness. Pomegranate seeds add tiny, refreshing bursts of intense pink, too.

Use any white fish you like, but I tend to use bream. It's not too expensive and has good texture and flavour. Get the fishmonger to fillet, skin and pin-bone your fish. Cod's good, too, as are sea bass and haddock. If you can buy it fresh enough, even pollack's just about acceptable.

Avocado prawns, ceviche-style

I far prefer those small, pink, comma-like North Atlantic prawns to the bland tiger prawns, often farmed in the East to ruinous environmental effect. If you can, buy them whole and peel. Every supermarket has them and even the cooked ones are OK. If you can find fresh ones, then all the better.

Put the prawns in a bowl with the lime juice, Tabasco and a big pinch of salt and pepper. Cover and leave in the fridge for 30 minutes. Mix in the onions, chillies and coriander. Serve in halved avocados. (Alternatively, mash the avocados, mix with the prawn ceviche and serve atop tortillas or stuffed into pitta bread).

{ SERVES 4 }

400 g/14 oz small cooked Atlantic prawns, peeled (or fresh, uncooked prawns)
juice of 1 lime
few drops of Tabasco
sea salt and freshly ground black pepper
2 red onions, finely chopped
6 bird's-eye chillies, finely chopped (or ½ habanero chilli if you want real heat, or a couple of standard green chillies if you really can't face heat, finely chopped)
small bunch of coriander, finely chopped
4 avocados

Bells of St Clement's ceviche

Seville orange juice, mixed 50:50 with lemon juice, gives a bitter-sweet edge to this dish, accentuated by ruby shards of pomegranate seeds. Substitute the Seville juice for normal orange with a good splash of grapefruit when Seville's out of season. Which is most of the year.

Slice the fish in 1 cm/½ inch-wide strips, then cut into dice. Place in a bowl and mix with the orange and lemon juices. Cover and leave in the fridge for 30 minutes, or until the fish is completely white and opaque.

Cut the pomegranate in half, hold over a plate, then whack the uncut side of each half with a rolling pin until the seeds drop out. Discard the white pith.

Mix the marinated fish with the pomegranate seeds, chillies, red onion, coriander and a big pinch of salt. Serve with tortilla chips.

{ SERVES 4 }

1 kg/2 lb 4 oz bass, filleted, skinned and pin-boned
juice of 2 Seville oranges (or 1 normal orange and ½ grapefruit)
juice of 1 lemon
1 ripe pomegranate
3 green finger chillies, or 3 jalapeños, or 1 Scotch bonnet, finely chopped
1 red onion, finely chopped
big handful of coriander, roughly chopped
sea salt
tortilla chips, to serve

Classic ceviche

{ SERVES 4 }

1 kg/2 lb 2 oz bream, filleted, skinned and pin-boned

juice of 2 limes

3 tomatoes, skinned, deseeded and finely diced

3 jalapeño chillies or 1 habanero, finely chopped (the latter is far hotter, but does have the most wonderful fruity depth)

1 red onion, finely chopped

big handful of coriander, finely chopped, plus extra sprigs to garnish

sea salt

4 soft tortillas, fried until crisp (optional), to serve

1 avocado, cut in half and sliced lengthways, to serve

Slice the fish into 1 cm/½ inch-wide strips, then cut into dice. Put in a bowl, mix with the lime juice and leave in the fridge, covered, for 30 minutes, or until the fish is completely white and opaque.

Gently mix in the diced tomatoes, chillies, onion, coriander and a big pinch of sea salt.

Serve (on fried tortillas, if you like) with slices of avocado and sprigs of coriander.

A trio of salsas

{ EACH RECIPE MAKES A BOWL FOR 6–8 }

No Mexican feast is complete without salsas, ranging from the fresh to the smoky to the fairly hot. You can then customise the taco to your own tastes.

Salsa pico de gallo

{ SERVES 6–8 }

2 white onions, finely chopped
5 tomatoes, skinned, deseeded and finely chopped
4 serrano chillies, finely chopped (or thin finger chillies if serranos are not available)
juice of 1 lime
sea salt
big handful of coriander, roughly chopped

The classic, crunchy all-purpose salsa, this is never far from the Mexican table. It's refreshing, too, perfect for cutting through some of the fattier local favourites.

Mix the onions, tomatoes, chillies and lime juice in a bowl; add salt to taste. Leave for an hour, add the coriander, then serve.

A roasted, fiery salsa

The habanero chilli is the main player here, so this is hot. But the roasted tomatoes add depth and a proper smoky tang.

{ SERVES 6–8 }

8 tomatoes, halved
sea salt and freshly ground black pepper
a splash of olive oil
4–12 habanero or Scotch bonnet chillies, stalks removed
3 tablespoons white wine vinegar

Preheat the oven to 200°C/400°F/Gas 6. Put the tomatoes on a baking tray, sprinkle with salt and pepper and a splash of olive oil and roast until the edges char and the tomatoes are soft: about 25 minutes.

Put the tomatoes in a blender, with the chillies, vinegar and a big pinch of salt. Blend until smooth.

A warm, smoky salsa

Heat and smoke. This is all about the chipotle, the smoked and dried jalapeño chilli.

{ SERVES 6–8 }

2 tablespoons groundnut oil
1 onion, finely chopped
2 cloves garlic, finely chopped
3–6 dried chipotle chillies, soaked in water for 15 minutes, drained and finely chopped
3 large tomatoes, skinned, deseeded and finely chopped
2 tablespoons white wine vinegar
pinch of dried oregano
pinch of caster sugar
sea salt and freshly ground black pepper

Heat the oil in a saucepan over a medium heat. Add the onion and garlic and soften for about 10 minutes, then add the chillies and cook for 2 minutes.

Add the tomatoes, vinegar, oregano, sugar and salt and pepper to taste and simmer gently for 20 minutes. Leave to cool before serving.

From far-flung shores

{ Sichuan food }

Ma. Nope, not some shrugging gesture of 'whatever'. Nor the smacking of lips. Rather the Sichuan term for 'numbing', a reaction caused by Sichuan peppers. They're small, red and dried, and have a wonderfully fragrant citrus tang. But when mixed with dried chillies, the effect becomes 'hot and numbing', perhaps the most famous facet of this regional Chinese cuisine.

Once upon a time, not so many years back, the UK was in thrall to Cantonese cooking. After all, most immigrants came from Hong Kong and southern China. And so we believed Chinese food was all about dim sum, delicate (or not-so-delicate) steamed fish and sweet-and-sour pork, unaware of the eight distinct culinary regions of that vast land.

Slowly, though, we're beginning to appreciate the various regions, as new restaurants open up. But it was Fuchsia Dunlop's brilliant *Sichuan Cookery* (Penguin 2001) that really got things going over here.

She was the first Westerner to learn to cook at the Sichuan Institute of Higher Cuisine in Chengdu. She taught us about a fascinating cuisine with 23 different flavour combinations, not all hot or numbing. 'Fish fragrant' is a fish-free combination of sweet, salty, sour and spicy. 'Scorched chilli' is best seen in a cucumber salad that manages to heat the tongue and cool the mouth simultaneously.

'China is the place for food,' goes the old saying, 'but Sichuan the place for flavour.'

Gong bao chicken

This Sichuan dish is better known, in the States at least, as *kung pao* chicken. But the versions I've tried are pretty drab, relying on peanuts and peppers rather than the elegant balance of ingredients that characterises the original. The key is to chop the chicken into similar-sized small cubes, so it cooks quickly and evenly.

Mix all the marinade ingredients in a bowl with 1 tablespoon water. Add the chicken, cover and leave to marinate in the fridge for 2 hours.

Make the sauce by mixing all the ingredients in a bowl or jug. Set aside.

When you are ready to cook the chicken, heat the groundnut oil in a wok until it is very hot but not smoking. Add the chillies and Sichuan peppercorns and stir-fry until crisp and fragrant, but don't let them burn.

Lift the chicken out of the marinade with a slotted spoon, add it to the pan and stir-fry over a high heat. Add a little marinade if it is too dry.

Once the chicken has turned white and firmed up, after about 2–3 minutes, add the spring onions, ginger and garlic, and stir-fry for a further 2 minutes; make sure the chicken is cooked through.

Add the sauce, stirring all the time. Once everything is thick and shiny, add the cashew nuts and serve with steamed rice.

{ SERVES 2 }

600 g/1 lb 5 oz chicken breast, cut into small cubes
2 tablespoons groundnut oil
6–30 Sichuan dried chillies
1½ tablespoons Sichuan peppercorns
7 spring onions, white parts only, cut on a diagonal
5 cm/2 inch piece of root ginger, thinly sliced using a vegetable peeler
4 cloves garlic, thinly sliced
70 g/2½ oz cashew nuts
steamed rice, to serve

For the marinade

5 teaspoons light soy sauce
2 teaspoons dark soy sauce
2 teaspoons Shaoxing rice wine
1½ teaspoons potato flour

For the sauce

2 teaspoons rice vinegar
3 tablespoons chicken stock
1 teaspoon caster sugar
1½ teaspoons potato flour
2 teaspoons light soy sauce
2 teaspoons dark soy sauce
6 teaspoons black Chinese vinegar
3 teaspoons sesame oil

Dan dan noodles

I first ate these not on the spice-scented streets of Chengdu, but in the rather less exotic environs of London's Soho. Barshu might not have been the first Sichuan restaurant to open in the capital but it is certainly the best. Sichuan's famed 'hot and numbing' flavour is based on chilli and the wonderfully citrus Sichuan pepper. This is a classic Sichuan street snack. If you can't find the preserved vegetables, don't worry.

Heat the oil in a wok over a medium heat. When it is hot but not smoking, add the chillies and Sichuan peppercorns and stir-fry briefly until the oil is fragrant. Take care not to burn the spices.

Add the *ya cai* or preserved vegetable and continue to stir-fry until hot and fragrant. Add the minced beef, splash in the soy sauce and stir-fry until the meat is brown and a little crisp, but not too dry. When the meat is cooked, remove the wok from the heat and set aside.

To make the sauce, combine the ingredients, divide between 2 serving bowls and mix well.

Cook the noodles according to the instructions on the packet. Drain them and add a portion to the sauce in each serving bowl. Sprinkle each bowl with the meat mixture and give the noodles a good stir until the sauce and meat are evenly distributed. Serve garnished with spring onions.

{ SERVES 2 }

1 tablespoon groundnut oil
3 Sichuan dried chillies, snipped in half, seeds discarded
½ teaspoon whole Sichuan peppercorns
25 g/1 oz Sichuan *ya cai* or *tianjin* preserved vegetable, thinly sliced
100 g/3½ oz minced beef
2 teaspoons light soy sauce
300 g/10½ oz dried Chinese noodles
spring onions, green part only, cut into thin rounds, to garnish

For the sauce

½–1 teaspoon ground roasted Sichuan peppercorns
1 tablespoon light soy sauce
1 tablespoon dark soy sauce
2 tablespoons chilli oil, with chilli sediment

From far-flung shores

Chicken chanko

{ SERVES 4 }

1 x 1.8 kg/4 lb chicken, boned – reserve the bones and cut the meat into 2.5 cm/1 inch chunks
4 large carrots
3 large leeks
2 large onions
8 peppercorns
125 ml/4 fl oz soy sauce
½ daikon (white radish or mooli)
½ Chinese cabbage
125 ml/4 fl oz sake
12 fresh shiitake mushrooms
400 g/14 oz fresh firm tofu, drained and diced, cut into 2.5 cm/1 inch cubes
sea salt
600 g/1 lb 5 oz fresh udon noodles

People tend to see Japanese food as endlessly light and elegant, all sushi, sashimi and artfully carved fruit. But this is just one part of the cuisine. Because Japan can get mighty cold in winter (except in the tropical south), so good, belly-lining tucker is desired. Think of *tonkatsu*, or breaded pork chop. And the sweetish curry rice, along with the ever-popular *ramen* (actually Chinese in origin), the ultimate in booze food. *Chankonabe*, better known as *chanko*, is a great filler, a chuck-it-all-in casserole devoured by sumo wrestlers, those great wobbling man-mountains. It's a communal, one-pot dish with simmering stock, into which is dipped chicken, pork, mushrooms, potatoes, carrots, onions, lotus root and pretty much anything else around. They're cooked and eaten, and the remaining stock is then drunk with rice and noodles. It's pretty hefty, but contains a minimal amount of fat. One particularly mighty sumo, Takamisugi, devoured 65 bowls in one sitting. He only stopped when his jaw began to hurt. 'If you wanna be a *rikishi* (sumo),' says the legendary Konishiki, 'you've gotta eat *chanko*.' And even if you don't harbour ambitions of slapping a multi-bellied beast from the chalk circle, it still makes for a good feasting dish.

Put the chicken bones in a large pot along with 1 quartered carrot, 1 quartered leek, 1 quartered onion, the peppercorns and the soy sauce. Cover with water, bring to the boil, skim, then simmer on a very low heat for 3 hours. Strain the

{ CONTINUES OVERLEAF }

From far-flung shores

stock into a large clean pan, skim again and place the pan of stock over the heat and bring to a simmer.

Cut the remaining carrots and leeks into 5 mm/¼ inch slices; cut the remaining onion in half, then slice thickly; cut the daikon into cubes. Blanch these vegetables for 2 minutes in the simmering stock, then remove with a slotted spoon and set aside.

Take 6 leaves of Chinese cabbage, blanch in the stock for 10 seconds, then remove, roll up the leaves and cut into 5 mm/¼ inch strips.

Add the chicken to the stock and simmer for 8–10 minutes. Return the leek and onion to the stock and cook for another minute. Add the carrots, daikon and sake and cook for a further minute, or until the chicken is cooked through.

Finally, add the mushrooms, tofu and cabbage and cook for 1 minute. Using a slotted spoon, scoop all the ingredients out of the stock into 4 bowls. Add the noodles to the stock and boil for a few minutes, until just tender. Ladle noodles and broth into the bowls. Eat, then lie down for a few hours, moaning softly.

Japanese aubergine

I could never get too excited about the aubergine. Interested, yes, but thrilled, no. That is until I tried a dish at Roka – one of the best contemporary Japanese restaurants in London – that made the taste buds swoon. It turns the aubergine into something soft, silken and wonderfully savoury.

{ SERVES 2 }

1 long Asian aubergine
  (a normal one is fine, too)
1 teaspoon vegetable oil
sea salt
2 tablespoons sweet white miso
1 tablespoon red miso
1 teaspoon caster sugar
2 tablespoons sake
2 tablespoons mirin
1 teaspoon soy sauce

Preheat the oven to 180°C/350°F/Gas 4.

Halve the aubergine lengthways and slash the flesh, not too deep, in a criss-cross pattern. Place on a baking sheet, brush with vegetable oil and season with salt, then bake for 15–20 minutes, turning over after 8 minutes, until golden but just firm.

Meanwhile, in a small pan, mix the white and red misos with the sugar, sake, mirin and soy sauce. Heat gently, stirring, until the sugar has dissolved and the liquid has reduced and thickened. Preheat the grill to high.

Remove the aubergine from the oven and paint the miso mixture all over the flesh side. Grill until the surface is scattered with black and golden spots.

Asian-style bass, John Dory, or other big white fish

This is a fusion dish of sorts, mixing wine and olive oil with soy sauce and rice vinegar. But it does work. You can use any white fish in this recipe, and either a whole fish, or fillets. As the flavours are strong, farmed bass is fine, though nowhere near wild bass. John Dory has exceptional sweetness, but it's best to buy it filleted, as there's a lot of bone.

If you have a whole fish, make 3 shallow diagonal cuts along one side of it using a sharp knife. Put it on a big piece of foil on a baking sheet, season it inside and out, and fill the belly with the lemon, garlic and chilli. (If using fillets, arrange them on a big piece of foil on a baking sheet, season and cover with the lemon, garlic and chilli.)

For the marinade, mix all the ingredients together. Pour the marinade over the fish, cover and leave in the fridge for an hour, turning once.

Preheat the oven to 200°C/400°F/Gas 6.

Fold the edges of the foil up to make a dish, then pour over the wine. Bake for 20-25 minutes, 10 minutes less for fillets. Test the fish is cooked before serving; it should flake easily when pressed with a knife.

{ SERVES 4}

1 bass (1.1 kg/2 lb 7½ oz), scaled and gutted, or the fillets from 2 John Dory
sea salt and freshly ground black pepper
1 lemon, sliced
1 clove garlic, thinly sliced
1 habanero chilli, thinly sliced (optional)
100 ml/3½ fl oz dry white wine

For the marinade
2 tablespoons light soy sauce
1 tablespoon dry white wine
2 tablespoons olive oil
1 teaspoon rice wine vinegar

Sisig (Filipino pork)

{ SERVES 6 }

1 kg/2 lb 2 oz pork belly (or 1 kg/2 lb 2 oz deboned pig's head meat: jowls, ears and cheek), cut into 1 cm/½ inch cubes
500 ml/18 fl oz pineapple juice
15 g/½ oz sea salt
10 g/¼ oz black peppercorns
6 chicken livers
2 large white onions, finely chopped
2 tablespoons lime juice, plus lime wedges to serve
4 tablespoons white vinegar
6–20 bird's-eye chillies, plus extra to serve
freshly ground black pepper

Filipino food is one of Asia's great hidden secrets. We 'go out' for a Thai green chicken curry, 'slurp' a Vietnamese *pho* and 'murder' a Chinese. Yet what about the food of the Philippines, a country that looks both east and west (thanks to over half a century of occupation by the Spanish and then Americans)? It's not as vivid and spicy as most Thai food, nor as delicate as Vietnamese. Vinegar is of huge importance, and many dishes tend towards the sweet. But I had a blast in Manila, an underloved and overlooked city. Sure, it ain't no looker. Dirty, chaotic and smog-filled. But it's got heart and soul and charm. This is a classic booze dish, and should use the whole of a pig's head. But I've adapted it to use pork belly. It's all about the contrast of textures: crisp, soft and crunchy. The citrus juice hews through the fat, the chillies add heat. It's one of the world's great dishes, and I ate endless versions. If you have a good butcher, ask him for a pig's head. Scorch off the hairs, then poach and debone so you're left with the ears, snout and all that wonderful cheek meat. I've adapted this recipe from one in *Kulinarya* (2008), a great guide to Philippine cuisine.

Put the pork belly (or head meat), pineapple juice, salt and peppercorns in a stockpot with 2 litres/3½ pints water. Cover and bring to the boil, then reduce to a simmer and cook for 1 hour.

{ CONTINUES OVERLEAF }

Heat a barbecue so the coals are glowing white-hot.

After 1 hour cooking, add the chicken livers to the pork and cook for a further 15 minutes, until the meat is fork-tender. Remove the pork and chicken livers from the pot and discard the liquid. Grill the pork over the hot charcoal, or fry over a high heat in a heavy-based pan, until the skin is brown and crisp.

Chop the chicken livers into small cubes, mix with the pork and place in a bowl. Mix in the onions, lime juice, vinegar and chillies. Season to taste with salt and pepper.

Heat a cast-iron griddle pan until white hot, then add the meat mixture. Cook for 3–5 minutes. This is the third cooking stage, where the meat becomes browner and crunchier still.

Serve sizzling hot, with cold beer, and extra chillies and lime wedges on the side.

Filipino beef stew (*Adobong baka*)

They say that *adobo* is the Filipino national dish. There are hundreds of versions, but it's actually a technique, meaning anything cooked in vinegar. I spent a week in and around Manila and two meals stand out. The first, in Pampanga, just north of the city, was with artist, chef and all-round Renaissance man Claude Tayag. He showed me that Filipino food was far more than the brown, greasy stereotype perpetuated across the world. We ate this *adobo* and *sinigang*: a sour, clear soup with seafood and all manner of other things. The second was dinner with the beautiful Margarita Fores and friends. There, we devoured some of the finest *lechon* (roasted suckling pig) I've tasted, with skin as thin and brittle as glazed caramel. Incredible.

{ SERVES 6 }

6 cloves garlic, finely chopped

½ teaspoon black peppercorns, crushed

125 ml/4 fl oz cane, palm or white wine vinegar

4 tablespoons soy sauce

2 bay leaves

1 kg/2 lb 2 oz beef short ribs or brisket, deboned and cut into 5 cm/2 inch cubes

4 tablespoons groundnut oil

sea salt

boiled white rice, to serve

In a large bowl, combine the garlic, peppercorns, vinegar, soy sauce and bay leaves. Add the beef, cover and marinate in the fridge for at least an hour; 6 hours would be better.

Preheat the oven to 150°C/300°F/Gas 2.

Remove the meat from the marinade. Heat 2 tablespoons of the oil in an ovenproof pan and brown the meat in batches over a high heat, adding extra oil as needed. Transfer to a plate and set aside. Add the marinade to the pan with 500 ml/18 fl oz water. Bring to the boil, then reduce to a simmer and add the beef, topping up with a little extra water if needed so the ribs are just covered.

Put the pan in the oven and cook for about 2–2½ hours, or until the meat is fork-tender. Season with salt to taste. Serve with rice and cold beer.

Goan mutton vindaloo

{ SERVES 6 }

6 cloves
5 cm/2 inch piece of cinnamon stick
10 peppercorns
½ star anise
1 teaspoon cumin seeds
1 teaspoon poppy seeds
15–20 dried red Kashmiri chillies, soaked in cold water for 15 minutes, drained
6 plump cloves garlic, finely chopped
2.5 cm/1 inch piece of root ginger, finely chopped
4 teaspoons cider vinegar
1 tablespoon tamarind pulp
800 g/1 lb 12 oz mutton (wether), cut into big chunks
4 tablespoons vegetable oil
3 onions, finely chopped
sea salt
½ teaspoon jaggery (or palm sugar), or to taste
15 curry leaves
handful of coriander, finely chopped
boiled basmati rice, to serve

Ah, vindaloo, that ultimate test of pungency prowess, a curry so fierce that it batters its way through the fizzy fug of a 12-pint night. Nice. The curry house version is about extreme, one-note heat; forget delicate spicing and subtle technique, this is basically a Madras (itself an English Indian invention) with an extra dose of chilli powder. I have to admit a fondness for this culinary bovver boy, but once you've tasted the real thing, there's no going back.

Vindaloo comes from Goa, the small coastal Indian state colonised by the Portuguese a few centuries back. Along with the English and Spanish, they were great seafarers and Empire builders, and actually introduced chillies to India. Mix this ingredient with pork preserved in vinegar and garlic (so it could last the long journey out at sea) and you have the basis for the dish. Vindaloo fuses the Portuguese word for wine (and by extension vinegar), *vin*, with *alhos*, or garlic. And as Goa was Christian, pork was permitted, while it was taboo in the rest of India. In time, the Portuguese wine vinegar was replaced with toddy, or the local palm vinegar. My version substitutes mutton for pork, but is equally good. Don't be put off by the long list of ingredients. You should have most of them anyway, and the actual cooking is very easy indeed.

Put the cloves, cinnamon, peppercorns, star anise, cumin and poppy seeds in a dry, heavy-based pan and roast over low–medium heat for a few minutes, until fragrant. Leave to cool, then grind using a pestle and mortar or an electric spice grinder.

Put the chillies, garlic, ginger, vinegar and tamarind into a blender and blitz until you have a smooth paste. Add the ground dry spices and blitz for a few seconds.

Use one-fifth of the spice paste to coat the mutton; cover and refrigerate for 30 minutes.

Meanwhile, heat the oil in a large casserole and fry the onions for 15–20 minutes, or until brown. Add the remaining spice paste and fry for a further 5 minutes, stirring continuously. Add a couple of tablespoons of water if the mixture starts to dry out.

Preheat the oven to 140°C/275°F/Gas 1.

Add the mutton to the pan and fry in the spice mixture for 5 minutes. Add 800 ml/1 pint 8 fl oz water, and season to taste with salt and jaggery. Cook in the oven for about 2½ hours, or until tender.

Stir in the curry leaves and simmer for 3–4 minutes. Then mix in the coriander and serve with basmati rice.

Rogan josh

{ SERVES 4 }

900 g/2 lb mutton chops
   (and 450 g/1 lb mutton bones,
   if you can get them)
2 teaspoons sea salt
150 g/5 oz Greek yogurt
1 tablespoon Kashmiri
   chilli powder
1 tablespoon paprika
4 tablespoons sunflower oil
450 g/1 lb shallots,
   finely chopped
6 cloves garlic, finely chopped
8 cloves
6 green cardamom pods,
   crushed
2 black cardamom pods, crushed
2 teaspoons fennel powder
large pinch of saffron strands
1 teaspoon grated nutmeg
1 teaspoon ground coriander
1 teaspoon ground ginger
4 bay leaves
small handful of coriander,
   roughly chopped, to serve
boiled basmati rice, to serve

This is a recipe from my friend Bill, a man whose love for India matches mine for Mexico and Thailand. I've travelled the globe with him on many occasions, and he's a trencherman in the truest form. Anyway, his take on the classic Kashmiri dish is wonderful. When buying mutton, ask for a wether (adolescent sheep) rather than an old boiler. The flavour is there but not overwhelming.

Put the chops and bones in a big saucepan, cover with 1.7 litres/3 pints water, add the salt, put the lid on and bring to the boil. Simmer for 30 minutes, then remove the chops, cover and put in the fridge. Discard the bones and skim off the scum from the liquid. Boil the stock over a high heat to reduce by half, about 20–30 minutes, and reserve.

Meanwhile, put the yogurt in a small bowl, add the chilli powder and paprika and whisk together; cover and set aside.

Heat 2 tablespoons of the oil in a frying pan and fry the shallots over a low heat for 15 minutes until nearly caramelised. Add the garlic, cloves and cardamom pods and fry for 2 minutes more. Remove from the heat and add the rest of the spices (but not the bay leaves). Stir in 2 tablespoons of the stock, then blitz to a paste in a blender or food processor.

Heat the rest of the oil in a casserole, then fry the chops over a medium–high heat for 2–3 minutes on each side, or until browned. Add the shallot paste, yogurt mixture, bay leaves and half the stock, bring gently to a simmer, cover and cook on a very low heat until the meat is tender, about 2 hours. Top up with stock if it becomes dry. Taste and add more salt if necessary. Serve, sprinkled with coriander, with basmati rice.

Yellow dhal

{ SERVES 4 WITH OTHER DISHES }

225 g/8 oz mung dhal (yellow split mung beans)
2 green chillies, roughly chopped
1 red chilli, roughly chopped
2 cm/¾ inch piece of root ginger, finely chopped
2 fresh or tinned tomatoes, roughly chopped
1 teaspoon cumin seeds, lightly toasted
3 cloves, crumbled
pinch of turmeric
2 teaspoons sea salt
4 cloves garlic, finely sliced
12 curry leaves
handful of fresh coriander, roughly chopped
3 spring onions, finely sliced
1 tablespoon sunflower oil

Indian comfort food at its best. You'll find this all over the north and central regions of the country. I remember having a version in a truck stop in Madhur Pradesh. As burly truckers snoozed on tattered *charpoys*, we dug in. I was expecting creamy comfort and got a dish so hot it nuked the roof of my mouth. But who says lentils are boring? They're far too good to leave for the hippies to muck up. A poached egg sat on top makes for a very civilised lunch.

Soak the mung dhal in water for 30 minutes, then drain and rinse. In a big saucepan, bring 1.2 litres/2 pints water to the boil. Add the mung dhal, chillies, ginger, tomatoes, cumin, cloves, turmeric, salt and half of the garlic. Bring to the boil, then boil for 10 minutes. Reduce the heat and simmer for a further 40 minutes, until the mung dhal soften and the mixture becomes almost soupy.

Using a stick blender or an egg whisk, beat until the dhal have mostly broken up keep a nubbly texture. Add the curry leaves, coriander and spring onions, then return to the heat for a couple of minutes. Remove from the heat and taste, adding more salt if necessary.

Heat the oil in a small frying pan and fry the rest of the garlic until light brown. Pour over the dhal, and serve.

Steamed fish, Cantonese-style

The Cantonese are obsessed with the freshest of fish. Hence those vast aquariums with gloomy-looking sea life, ready to be fished out to order. This is a simple dish, so much depends on the quality of the fish. You can use a dedicated fish steamer, a large bamboo basket, or even a colander inside a wok (make sure the bottom of the colander doesn't touch the water).

Rinse and dry the fish, inside and out. Make 3 shallow diagonal cuts into each side of it and rub with salt. Rub a little into the cavity, too. Put the fish on a heatproof platter and scatter with the ginger.

Fill the steamer or wok with about 5 cm/2 inches of water and bring to the boil. Put the fish platter into the steamer or wok, cover and steam for 20 minutes or more, depending on the size of the fish. The fish should be opaque, and flake easily away from the bone.

Remove the fish platter and pour off any excess liquid, then pour over the soy sauces.

In a small pan, heat both oils together until they begin to shimmer, then pour over the fish and top with spring onions. Serve with steamed rice.

{ SERVES 2 }

1 x 600 g–1 kg/1 lb 5 oz–2 lb 2 oz, very fresh, firm-fleshed white fish, such as bass, sole or snapper, gutted and scaled but head on
big pinch of salt
5 cm/2 inch piece of root ginger, cut into long shreds
3 tablespoons light soy sauce
1 tablespoon dark soy sauce
2 teaspoons sesame oil
1 tablespoon groundnut oil
5 spring onions, shredded
steamed rice, to serve

{ Cooking for children }

I'm not a nutritionist or dietitian. Thank God, because the vast majority talk crap. There are good ones, though, sensible and pragmatic. Once my daughter Lola moved onto solid food, at around five months, I panicked. I couldn't use salt, or spice, or chilli, the basis of most things I cook. But I took recipes from Annabel Karmel (someone I do rate) and Mark Hix's *Eat Up: Food for Children of All Ages* (Fourth Estate, 2003) and adapted them as time went on.

For me, fresh food always best. You don't want any salt in the first year or so – and keep it low after that. But anything is better than those dreary ready-made pots. However posh or organic or free-range they profess to be, they all taste exactly the same: over-sweet and deathly dull.

I've never cooked anything I wouldn't eat myself for my children. Not that I'd want to exist solely on apple purée or chicken and carrots. All these recipes have proper flavour.

I tended to make big batches of dishes once a week, then freeze them in small pots. A stick blender was an essential accessory (for the first year, mush is order of the day) and a steamer, too. Both my children can be fussy, and usually prefer a bag of Quavers or packet of Haribo to a lovingly prepared lunch. There's nothing wrong with treats. It's only when junk becomes the mainstay of a child's diet that things go wrong. Mine both go through stages: one loving pasta and tomato sauce, the other hating it. I try not to force food on my children, but, on the other hand, they play us like pros. Balance, pragmatism and patience are key.

Big beefy stew

{ MAKES 10 PORTIONS }

40 g/1½ oz unsalted butter
2 tablespoons olive oil
500 g/1 lb 2 oz braising or chuck steak, fat removed, cut into 4 cm/1½ inch cubes
3 small onions, finely chopped
6 carrots, finely chopped
400 g/14 oz sweet potatoes, peeled and cut into 4 cm/1½ inch cubes
250 g/9 oz button mushrooms, sliced
juice of 2 oranges
2 sprigs of thyme
400 ml /14 fl oz unsalted vegetable or chicken stock, or water
40 g/1½ oz spinach

Forget what those idiotic health fascists have to say about red meat. A young child needs it. This is stewed until it falls apart into wonderfully tender strands. Our old friend the sweet potato adds sweetness, as do the ubiquitous carrots.

Preheat the oven to 140°C/275°F/Gas 1. In a casserole, heat the butter with the oil and brown the meat in batches over a highish heat; remove the meat and set aside. Reduce the heat to medium.

Add the onions to the casserole and soften for about 5 minutes, then add the carrots, sweet potatoes and mushrooms and cook for a further 5 minutes. Return the meat to the pan and add the orange juice, thyme and stock or water.

Bring to the boil, then cover the casserole and cook in the oven for 3 hours, or until the meat is tender. Add the spinach 15 minutes before the end of the cooking time.

Blitz until smooth if necessary to suit your child (adjust the consistency with boiled water if needed).

Spaghetti bollynaise

You can't fail with this classic, the mainstay of my youth. The real difference between this and my other version (see pages 165-167) is less salt and no booze. When my children were younger, I'd use the small stars rather than spaghetti, as they're easier to eat.

Heat the oil in a big saucepan over a medium heat and soften the onion for 5 minutes. Add the carrots, celery and garlic and cook until soft, another 10 minutes. Turn up the heat, add the beef and brown, stirring, for about 5 minutes.

Add the tomatoes, tomato purée, Worcestershire sauce and stock. Bring to the boil, then simmer, covered, on a low heat for 30–40 minutes, stirring from time to time and breaking up the mince with a wooden spoon.

Boil the pasta following the packet instructions. Blitz the sauce until smooth if necessary to suit your child and serve with pasta and grated Parmesan.

{ MAKES 8 PORTIONS }

1 tablespoon olive oil
1 large onion, finely chopped
3 carrots, finely chopped
3 celery stalks, finely chopped
2 cloves garlic, finely chopped
500 g/1 lb 2 oz minced beef
400 g/14 oz tomatoes, skinned and chopped, or 1 x 400g/14 oz tin of chopped tomatoes
2 teaspoons tomato purée
1 tablespoon Worcestershire sauce
300 ml/½ pint unsalted stock or water
pasta stars or spaghetti, to serve
freshly grated Parmesan, to serve

Chicken à la Lola

{ **MAKES ABOUT 10 PORTIONS** }

25 g/1 oz unsalted butter
2 small onions, roughly chopped
2 large carrots, cut into small cubes
1 sweet potato, peeled and cut into small cubes
200 g/7 oz chicken breast (the best you can afford), cut into 2.5 cm/1 inch cubes
big handful of spinach
mashed potato or cooked pasta, to serve

This was one of the first dishes I cooked for my daughter Lola. It's packed with all sorts of worthy ingredients, and I added sweet potato (one tuber I've never really got the hang of) and carrot for an extra allure.

Melt the butter in a saucepan, add the onions and soften over a medium heat for about 5 minutes.

Add the carrots and sweet potato and cook gently for another 5 minutes. Add the chicken and cook, stirring, until it is white.

Add 250 ml/9 fl oz water, bring to the boil, then simmer, covered, for 20 minutes, or until the chicken is cooked through. Add the spinach and cook for 2–3 minutes more, until wilted.

Blitz until smooth if necessary to suit your child (adjust the consistency with boiled water if needed). For older children, just serve up as it is, with mashed potato or pasta.

Coriander chicken

I used to despise fresh coriander… literally couldn't look at the stuff. And, like the *Princess and the Pea*, I could detect even the tiniest leaf. This made Thai food a bore, and Indian, too. One day, though, I fell in love. Just like that. Now I couldn't live without its idiosyncratically metallic charms. I thought I'd try it out on Lola when she was young, to see what she thought. And she loved it. That said, at the age she is now, she declares love for one thing only to disown it the next day.

Melt the butter in a saucepan, add the onion and soften over a medium heat for about 5 minutes.

Add the carrots and cook for a further 5 minutes, then add the chicken and cook, stirring, until it is white. Add the coriander and watercress and cook for another minute.

Add the stock or water, bring to the boil, then turn down the heat and simmer, covered, for 20 minutes, or until the chicken is cooked through.

Blitz until smooth if necessary to suit your child (adjust the consistency with boiled water if needed).

{ **MAKES 12 PORTIONS** }

50 g/1¾ oz unsalted butter

1 large onion, finely chopped

8 carrots, cut into small cubes

3 chicken breasts (the best you can afford), cut into 2.5 cm/1 inch cubes

big handful of coriander leaves, roughly chopped

big handful of watercress, roughly chopped

400 ml/14 fl oz unsalted stock or water

Chick 'n' carrots

{ MAKES 8 PORTIONS }

25 g/1 oz unsalted butter
2 small onions, roughly chopped
7 carrots, cut into small cubes
2 chicken breasts (the best you can afford), cut into 2.5 cm/1 inch cubes
85 g/3 oz spinach
300 ml/½ pint unsalted stock or water

Another chicken creation, with all sorts of goodness hidden within.

Melt the butter in a saucepan, add the onions and soften over a medium heat for about 5 minutes.

Add the carrots and cook for another 5 minutes, then add the chicken and cook, stirring, until it is white. Add the spinach and cook for 2–3 minutes more, until wilted.

Add the stock or water, bring to the boil, then turn down the heat and simmer, covered, for 20 minutes, or until the chicken is cooked through.

Blitz until smooth if necessary to suit your child (adjust the consistency with boiled water if needed).

Lola's favourite liver

OK, it doesn't sound too appetising, but Lola used to adore this. And all that iron is a good thing. Bacon adds more flavour, as does sage.

Put the potatoes in a pan of cold water, bring to the boil, then simmer until soft, about 15 minutes. Drain, return to the pan and leave to steam dry for 10 minutes. Mix in the butter and milk, then pass through a ricer and set aside. (Do not blitz the mashed potato in a blender or food processor or it will become like glue.)

Meanwhile, heat the oil in a frying pan over a medium heat, add the onion and bacon and cook until the onion is soft and bacon golden, about 5 minutes. Add the livers and fry for 2 minutes, until just browned. Add the sage and thyme, then 150 ml/¼ pint water, and simmer for 2 minutes, until the liver is cooked.

Blitz the liver mixture if necessary to suit your child, then mix with the mash.

{ MAKES 6 PORTIONS }

750 g/1 lb 10 oz floury potatoes, peeled and cubed
25 g/1 oz unsalted butter
2–3 tablespoons full-fat milk
1 tablespoon olive oil
1 small onion, finely chopped
3 rashers unsmoked back bacon, soaked in cold water for an hour to remove salt and drained if making this for infants, then roughly chopped
250 g/9 oz chicken livers, cleaned and roughly chopped
4 sage leaves, roughly chopped
big pinch of thyme, roughly chopped

Cooking for children

Fish pie jr

{ MAKES 8 MINI PIES }

1 kg/2 lb 2 oz floury potatoes, peeled and cubed
400 ml/14 fl oz full-fat milk, plus 2–3 tablespoons for the mash
150 g/5½ oz unsalted butter
2 onions, roughly chopped
4 tomatoes, skinned, deseeded and roughly chopped
2 tablespoons plain flour
450 g/1 lb cod fillet, skinned, pin-boned and cut into small chunks
450 g/1 lb salmon fillet, skinned, pin-boned and cut into small chunks
2 tablespoons finely chopped parsley
1 bay leaf
100 g/3½ oz Cheddar, grated
1 egg, lightly beaten

I use salmon and cod for this, but you can substitute haddock, pollack or whatever. As the children get older, I tend to add good smoked haddock, too.

Put the potatoes in a pan of cold water, bring to the boil, then simmer until soft, about 15 minutes. Drain, add 2–3 tablespoons milk and half the butter, and mash until it is smooth.

Preheat the oven to 180°C/350°F/Gas 4.

Melt rest of the butter in a heavy-based pan over a medium heat and soften the onions for 5 minutes. Add the tomatoes and cook for another couple of minutes, then stir in the flour and cook for a further minute.

Add the milk, bring to the boil and cook, stirring, for a minute. Then add the fish, parsley and bay leaf and simmer for 5 minutes, stirring from time to time, until the fish is just cooked. Remove the bay leaf, add the cheese and stir until melted.

Divide the fish mixture between 8 ramekins, top with mashed potato and brush with beaten egg. Bake for 15–20 minutes, until the potato is golden and the fish mixture bubbling and piping-hot.

Salmon with carrots & tomatoes

Buy the best farmed salmon you can afford. It keeps well in the freezer. Cheese adds more flavour, as the fish can tend towards the bland. Do make sure you remove any errant bones.

Steam the carrots for 15 minutes.

Meanwhile, put the salmon in a saucepan, cover with the milk and simmer gently for 6 minutes, until cooked. Drain and set aside, reserving the milk.

Melt the butter in a pan over a low heat, add the tomatoes and cook until mushy. Add the cheese and cook until melted, then blitz with the carrots until you have a coarse mash. Flake the fish and add to the tomato and cheese mixture.

Blitz until smooth if necessary to suit your child (adjust the consistency with some of the reserved poaching milk if needed).

{ MAKES 8 PORTIONS }

6 carrots, cut into small cubes
300 g/10½ oz salmon fillet, skinned and pin-boned
200 ml/7 fl oz milk
40 g/1½ oz unsalted butter
4 ripe tomatoes, skinned, deseeded and roughly chopped
100 g/3½ oz Cheddar, grated

Cooking for children

Fishcakes

{ MAKES 16 SMALL OR 8 LARGE FISHCAKES }

300 g/10½ oz cod, skinned and pin-boned
300 g/10½ oz salmon, skinned and pin-boned
300 ml/½ pint full-fat milk
3 rashers unsmoked back bacon, soaked in cold water for an hour to remove salt and drained if making this for infants
600 g/1 lb 5 oz floury potatoes, peeled and cubed
15 g/½ oz unsalted butter
2 teaspoons tomato ketchup
1 teaspoon English mustard
2 tablespoons finely chopped flat-leaf parsley
freshly ground black pepper
plain flour, for dusting
2–4 tablespoons olive oil

Lots of fishy goodness packed in here, with the bacon adding a touch of depth and smoke. The children both gobble up every last morsel. A rare sight indeed.

Put the fish in a pan, add the milk and poach for 4 minutes. Drain and flake the fish, reserving the milk. Set aside.

Fry the bacon until crisp; chop into small pieces and set aside.

Put the potatoes in a pan of cold water, bring to the boil, then simmer until soft, about 15 minutes. Drain, return to the pan and leave to steam dry for 10 minutes. Mix in the butter and a good splash of the reserved poaching milk, then pass through a ricer and set aside.

Mix the mashed potato with the fish, bacon, ketchup, mustard, parsley and pepper.

Shape into small balls, flatten, then leave to rest in the fridge, covered, for 1 hour on a baking sheet.

Dust the fishcakes very lightly with flour. Heat a little olive oil in a frying pan over a high heat and fry the fishcakes in batches until crisp and golden and cooked right through.

Cheesy pasta

This really is an emergency fallback, needing just pasta, butter, Parmesan and Cheddar. If you're lacking one cheese, use more of the other.

Cook the pasta as directed on the packet. Drain.

Melt butter on the hot pasta and add the cheeses, mixing quite hard. Add pepper and serve immediately.

{ SERVES 2 }

85 g/3 oz baby pasta or spaghetti
40 g/1½ oz unsalted butter
handful of grated Parmesan
handful of grated Cheddar
freshly ground black pepper

Tomato & veg pasta sauce

{ MAKES 10 PORTIONS }

4 medium carrots, sliced
425 g/15 oz cauliflower, cut into florets, woody core discarded
100 g/3½ oz unsalted butter
1 kg/2 lb 4 oz tomatoes, skinned, deseeded and roughly chopped
200 g/7 oz Cheddar, grated
baby pasta, to serve

Full of carefully hidden vegetables.

Steam the carrots and cauliflower for 7 minutes.

Melt the butter in a saucepan and cook the tomatoes over a medium heat for 5 minutes. Add the cheese and stir until melted. Boil the pasta following the packet instructions and drain.

Blitz the tomato and cheese mixture with the veg. Serve with the pasta.

Lentil salad

It's bad enough trying to force lentils down the throats of grown men, let alone squealing children. But lentils, cooked well (i.e. not into a muddy mush) are a noble ingredient: cheap, easy to store and possessed of a wonderfully nutty, earthy taste. I particularly like those tiny greenish-brown ones from Puy in France, but most are OK. Wash first, to remove any unwelcome stones and twigs, then cook at a simmer for anything from 25 minutes to an hour. You want them al dente. This recipe was born in Sicily when I was cooking for about eight children. They were bored with pasta, as we'd had the stuff day in and day out for the past two weeks. So I just gathered together what was close to hand. For adults, add chilli and more salt.

{ SERVES 8 }

500 g/1 lb 2 oz Puy lentils, rinsed
1 onion, halved, plus 2 onions, finely chopped
1 clove garlic, peeled, plus 2–3 cloves garlic, finely chopped
2 bay leaves
2 tablespoons olive oil, plus 4 tablespoons extra-virgin olive oil for the dressing
350 g/12 oz tomatoes, skinned, deseeded and chopped
big handful of flat-leaf parsley, finely chopped
sea salt and freshly ground black pepper
2–3 tablespoons white-wine vinegar

Put the lentils in a big saucepan along with the halved onion, whole garlic clove and the bay leaves. (Do not salt the water, as this can make the skins tough.) Bring to the boil, then reduce to a simmer; the lentils may take anything from 25–60 minutes, so keep tasting; they're done when they're still firm, but with a little give. Drain, remove the onion, garlic and bay leaves and set aside.

Heat 2 tablespoons olive oil in a frying pan and soften the chopped onions and garlic over a medium heat for 10 minutes, then mix with lentils.

Add the tomatoes and parsley to the lentils and mix, then season to taste (you'll need salt unless cooking for very young children), and throw in the olive oil and vinegar. Serve.

Cooking for children

Lunch from a late summer English garden

{ MAKES 8 PORTIONS }

2 chicken breasts (the best you can afford), cut into small dice
juice of 1 lime
2 teaspoons of honey
a splash of reduced salt soy sauce
25 g/1 oz unsalted butter
1 tablespoon olive oil
4 small red onions, finely chopped
6 small courgettes, diced
4 small carrots, diced
8 rashers unsmoked streaky bacon or pancetta, soaked in cold water for an hour to remove salt and drained if making this for infants, diced
300 ml/ ½ pint reduced salt chicken stock or water
freshly ground black pepper
boiled rice or new potatoes, to serve

Every August we go down to my mother's house in the country for a week or so. If the weather's good, life's good. Less so if it's dreary and drizzling. My mother's kitchen garden, though, is incredible. One day, I walked through with a basket, picking whatever looked good – tiny red onions, elegant carrots, baby courgettes and endless herbs.

Put the chicken in a bowl, add the lime juice, honey and soy sauce, cover and marinate in the fridge for 2 hours.

Melt the butter and oil in a big saucepan, add the onions and soften over a low–medium heat for about 5 minutes. Add the courgettes and carrots. Increase the heat to medium-high, add the bacon and fry until just crisp, then reduce the heat, add the chicken, reserving the marinade, and cook for 5 minutes.

Add the reserved marinade, stock or water, a little pepper to taste and simmer for a further 10 minutes, or until the chicken is cooked through. Serve with boiled rice or new potatoes.

Red sauce for pasta

There's always some of this sauce in the deep freeze and when supplies start to dwindle, the only work involved is chopping a few onions and cloves of garlic. As for the basil, I bought a plant in Tesco a year back, re-potted it and it sits at the kitchen window, flourishing.

Heat the oil in a big saucepan over a low–medium heat and soften the onion and garlic for 10 minutes.

Add the tomato purée and cook for a minute, then add the tomatoes and sugar and stir. Add a generous grinding of black pepper, then simmer gently for 40 minutes, stirring from time to time, until thickened.

Boil the pasta following the packet instructions.

Remove the sauce from the heat and stir in the basil and Parmesan. Serve with the pasta.

{ MAKES 16 PORTIONS }

2 tablespoons olive oil
1 large onion, finely chopped
2 cloves garlic, finely chopped
2 teaspoons tomato purée
800 g/1 lb 12 oz tomatoes, skinned, deseeded and chopped, or 2 x 400g/14 oz tins chopped tomatoes
pinch of caster sugar
freshly ground black pepper
handful of basil, roughly chopped
handful of grated Parmesan
pasta or baby pasta, to serve

Cooking for children

Veggie mess

{ MAKES 6 PORTIONS }

2 sweet potatoes, peeled and cut into 1 cm/½ inch cubes
8 carrots, sliced
1 cauliflower, cut into florets, woody core discarded
40 g/1½ oz spinach

This purée has a good flavour and is, of course, packed with veggie goodness.

Steam the sweet potatoes and carrots for 10 minutes, then blitz until smooth (adjust the consistency with boiled water if needed) and set aside.

Steam the cauliflower for 10 minutes, adding the spinach for last 2 minutes. Blitz until smooth (again, adjust the consistency with boiled water if needed). Add to the sweet potato and carrot purée and mix.

Cupcakes

I can't bear these gaudy, over-sweet confections, and this is one craze that has entirely passed me by. My daughter, though, disagrees and is obsessed with the things. So we spent an afternoon making the cake batter, baking, then decorating, and she was in utter heaven. I enjoyed myself, too, and it's become a regular, if messy, way to spend a wet Saturday afternoon. I've gone for a pink-tinted white chocolate icing, but you can use any colour you like. As for decorations – edible silver balls, hundreds and thousands, Smarties, Rolos, edible glitter – the choice is relentless.

Preheat the oven to 180°C/350°F/Gas 4. Line a 12-hole cupcake tin with paper cases.

Put the flour, cocoa powder, sugar and butter into a food processor and blend until mixed. Add half the milk and blend briefly to mix.

In a bowl, whisk the remaining milk with the egg and vanilla extract. Beat for 30 seconds, then pour into the flour mixture and blend until just smooth – but do not overmix.

Spoon into the paper cases, filling about two-thirds full. Bake for 15–20 minutes, until pale golden and the cakes spring back when you touch them lightly. Allow to cool on a wire rack.

For the icing, mix the butter and icing sugar in a food processor until smooth. Transfer to a bowl and gradually fold in the melted chocolate (it should be barely warm), vanilla seeds and food colouring. Cool in the fridge for 20–30 minutes.

Using an icing bag or palette knife, cover the cakes with icing. Decorate – or let your children take over. Leave to set.

{ **MAKES 12** }

100 g/3½ oz self-raising flour, sifted
25 g/1 oz cocoa powder, sifted
140 g/5 oz caster sugar
40 g/1½ oz butter, at room temperature
125 ml/4 fl oz milk
1 large egg
½ teaspoon vanilla extract
edible glitter, hundreds and thousands, chocolate buttons, Smarties, etc, to decorate

For the icing
125 g/4½ oz butter, at room temperature
125 g/4½ oz icing sugar, sifted
125 g/4½ oz white chocolate, melted
seeds scraped from ½ vanilla pod
1 drop pink food colouring (or any colour you fancy)

Chocolate chip cookies

{ MAKES 12–15 }

115 g/4 oz butter, softened, plus extra for greasing
70 g/2½ oz caster sugar
1 medium egg yolk
2 drops vanilla extract
150 g/5½ oz plain flour, sifted
40 g/1½ oz chocolate chips, either posh chocolate or something good such as Dairy Milk, smashed into pieces

This is a recipe from Caroline, my mother-in-law, and it's a cracker. The cookies are so easy that Lola can bake them. Usually rather better than I.

Preheat the oven to 180°C/350°F/Gas 4. Grease a large baking tray with butter.

In a large bowl, cream the butter, sugar, egg yolk and vanilla extract with a wooden spoon.

Add the flour gradually, stirring to make thick dough. Then stir in the chocolate chips.

Scoop out a dessertspoon of dough at a time, mould into a ball and place on the greased baking tray. Press with your fingertips to flatten into biscuit shapes. Leave plenty of space between each biscuit.

Bake for 12–15 minutes, until lightly golden but still a little soft in the middle. Let them cool a little before eating. Easier said than done.

Index

Pages with illustrations have page numbers in italic

achiote paste 214
Affogato 141
Albert, Matthew 200
ancho chillies 152, 193
anchovies, Purple-sprouting broccoli with chillies & 116, *117*
asparagus
 in Baked eggs 54
 Griddled, with duck egg 113
 Jeremy's baked asparagus 114
Atherton, Jason 89
aubergine, Japanese aubergine 235
Autumn pudding *84*, *85*
avocado
 Avocado prawns, ceviche-style 221
 in Classic ceviche 224
 in Guacamole 216

bacon
 in Boeuf Bourguignon 160
 in Boeuf en daube *158*, *159*
 in Fishcakes – good for all ages 258
 in Lola's favourite liver 255
 in Lunch from a late summer English garden 262
 in Rabbit & cider casserole *188*, 189
 in Roast woodcock 25
 Smoked eel & bacon salad 124, *125*
 in The perfect burger 23
 see also pancetta
banana chilli 192
banana leaves 214
Bangkok, street food 196-7
barbecue
 Proper ribs 172, *173*
 Pulled pork *176*, 177, *178*
Barshu (Sichuan restaurant) 231
basil
 Orange, red onion & basil salad 132
 Minced beef with chillies & basil 201
Baxter's soups 170
beans
 broad beans *in* Fennel & orange salad 130, *131*
 in Green papaya salad 206
 Provençal green bean salad 127
 red kidney beans (canned) 154
Beaufort cheese, *in* French onion soup 60, *61*
beef
 Beef Stroganoff 22
 Big beefy stew 250
 Boeuf Bourguignon 160
 Boeuf en daube 158, *159*
 Braised ox cheeks 169
 Carbonade flamande 164

Filipino beef stew (*Adobong baka*) 241
 Home-made salt beef 162
 Mexican beef stew 210, *211*
 Oxtail stew 168
 Pot-au-feu 156
 Stir-fried beef with cumin 200
 Thai beef salad *198*, 199
 see also steak
beef (minced)
 in Chilli cottage pie 20
 in James's 'Old Bank' chili 155
 Minced beef with chillies & basil 201
 in Ragù alla Bolognese 165
 in Spaghetti Bollynaise 251
 in Spaghetti with meatballs 18, *19*
 in The perfect burger 23
beer, ale and stout
 in Braised ox cheeks 169
 in Carbonade flamande 164
 in English rabbit 136
Beeton, Mrs 133
Bigelow, Kathryn, *Point Break* 18
bird's-eye chillies 30, 93, 129, 154, 180, 192, 197, 202, 203, 204, 206, 207, 221, 238
biscuits, Chocolate chip cookies 266, *267*
blackberries, *in* Autumn pudding *84*, *85*
Blackface Meat Company, The 25
Bloody Mary 147
Blumenthal, Heston 66
Bradley Smoker 174, 177
Brass Rail (salt-beef bar) 162
bread
 in Autumn pudding *84*, *85*
 baguettes 60
 with Potted shrimps 49
Bread sauce 28
breadcrumbs, fried 26
bream, *in* ceviche 220, 224, *225*
Bridget (cook) 78
Brillat-Savarin 133
broccoli *in* Oriental cucumber salad *128*, 129
broccoli (purple-sprouting), with chillies & anchovies 116, *117*
broths
 Chicken, lime & lemongrass soup 204, *205*
 Chicken stock 39
 Shrimp broth 207
 see also soups and consommés
Brown & Forrest Smokery 124
Brussels sprouts, *in* stock 71
Buñuel, Luis 143
burger, The perfect burger 23
Buys, Caroline 266
Byron's burger chain, 23

cabbage
 Chinese cabbage *in* Chicken *chanko* 232

Chinese cabbage *with* Green papaya salad 206
 with Rabbit & cider casserole *188*, 189
Caerphilly cheese, *in* Aligot 70
Cantonese-style, Steamed fish 247
Carluccio, Antonio 64, 115
 A Passion for Mushrooms 137
carrots
 Chick 'n' carrots 254
 Salmon with carrots & tomatoes 257
 in Tomato & veg pasta sauce 260
 in Veggie mess 264
casseroles
 Boeuf Bourguignon 160
 Boeuf en daube 158, *159*
 Braised ox cheeks 169
 Rabbit and cider casserole *188*, 189
 see also pot-au-feu; stews
cauliflower, *in* Tomato & veg pasta sauce 260
caviar, Baked potatoes with caviar 48
ceviche, 220-25
 Avocado prawns, ceviche-style 221
 Bells of St Clement's ceviche *222*, *223*
 Classic ceviche 224, *225*
Cheddar cheese
 in Cauliflower cheese 62
 in Cheesy pasta 259
 in Crab toasts 135
 in English rabbit 136
 in Fish pie jr 256
 with Salmon, carrots & tomatoes 257
 with Tomato & veg pasta sauce 260
Chengdu (Sichuan) 228
Chesterton, G K 13
Chiang Mai (Thailand) 197
chicken
 A deeply healthy, utterly addictive noodle dish 30, *31*
 A simple dish for bachelors and widowers to impress their guests *102*, 103
 Chick 'n' carrots 254
 Chicken *chanko* 232, *233*
 Chicken, lime & lemongrass soup 204, *205*
 Chicken à la Lola 252
 Chicken & mushroom pie *36*, 37
 Chicken stock 38, 39
 Chicken & sweetcorn soup 33
 Coriander chicken 253
 Gong bao chicken 229
 Larp gai (Laotian chicken salad) 203
 in Lunch from a late summer English garden 262
 in Mole *verde* 217, *219*
 My mother's roast chicken 34, *35*
 in Oriental cucumber salad *128*, 129
 Pot-roast chicken 29

chicken livers
    Chicken liver & chorizo salad 120, *121*
    Lola's favourite liver 255
    in Ragù alla Bolognese 165
    in Sisig (Filipino pork) 238, *239*
Chile Pepper Magazine 192
Chillies 192-3, *194-5*
    with Asian steak in lettuce 93
    Chilli cottage pie 20
    Cumin & chilli paste 200
    gochujang chilli paste 30, 32, 129
    harissa chilli paste 154
    in Home-made salt beef 162
    Kashmiri chillies 242, 244
    Minced beef with chillies & basil 201
    in Oriental cucumber salad *128*, 129
    in Penne *all'amatriciana* 180, *181*
    Purple-sprouting broccoli with chillies & anchovies 116, *117*
    Sichuan chillies 229
    Tom's 10-alarm chili 152, *153*
    with Yellow dhal 246
    see also chilli types by name
China
    influence on Thai food 197
    see also Cantonese-style; Sichuan dishes
chipotle chillies 152, 192, 210, 227
Chocolate & orange soufflés 86, *87*
chorizo
    Chicken liver & chorizo salad 120, *121*
    chorizo scrambled eggs 52, *53*
Churchill, [Sir] Winston 143
cider
    Hot cider punch 142
    Rabbit & cider casserole *188*, 189
Cochinita pibil 214
cocktails 143-7
    Bloody Mary 147
    Bullshot 170
    Dry martini 143, 144, *145*
    Negroni 146
cod 220
    in A really good fish pie 40, *41*
    in ceviche 220
    in Fishcakes – good for all ages 258
    in Fish pie jr 256
    in goujons 46, *47*
coffee (espresso), *in* Affogato 141
Coriander chicken 253
Corrigan, Richard 14
cottage pie, Chilli 20
Coulson, Francis 72
courgettes, *in* Lunch from a late summer English garden 262
Crab toasts 135
cream cheese, *in* Kipper pâté 108
cream (double cream)
    in Ragù alla Bolognese 165
    in Rhubarb fool 138, *139*
cream (soured cream) 210, 212
Crowden, James, *Ciderland* 142
crumble, Rhubarb & ginger 83
cucumber
    Cucumber raita 98, *99*
    Oriental cucumber salad *128*, 129

Cumin & chilli paste 200
cumin seeds
    Stir-fried beef with cumin 200
Cupcakes 265
curry, Goan mutton vindaloo 242
custard 75

daikon (white radish or mooli) *in* Chicken *chanko* 232, *233*
Dan dan noodles *230*, 231
David, Elizabeth 159
del Conte, Anna 165
desserts *see* puddings
dhal
    Yellow dhal 246
    see also lentils
Drinks 142-7
Dry martini 143, 144, *145*
Dunlop, Fuchsia, *Sichuan Cookery* 228

Eccles cake ice cream 82
Eccles cakes 80
eel *see* smoked eel
eggs 50
    Baked eggs 54
    in Chocolate & orange soufflés 86, *87*
    Chorizo scrambled eggs 52, *53*
    in custard 75
    Fried eggs 55
    fried egg, *with* Minced beef with chillies & basil 201
    Griddled asparagus with poached duck egg 113
    in Huevos rancheros 57
    in Mayonnaise 59
    poached, *in* Haddock Parker Bowles 43, *45*
    poached, *with* Yellow dhal 246
    Scrambled eggs ('Gegs (9-4)') 58
    in Spaghetti alla carbonara 96
    Tortilla 56
Elie, Lolis Eric, *Smokestack Lightning* 171
Emmental cheese, *with* French onion soup 60, *61*
endive (curly), *in* Smoked eel & bacon salad 124, *125*
Escoffier, Auguste 156

fat, cooking with 16
Fearnley-Whittingstall, Hugh, *The River Cottage Meat Book* 25
fennel
    in Cos & haddock salad 123
    Fennel & orange salad 130, *131*
feuilles de brick, *in* Jeremy's baked asparagus 114
fish *see* individual fish by name
fish pie, A really food fish pie 40, *41*
Fish pie jr 256
Fish (steamed), Cantonese-style 247
Fishcakes – good for all ages 258
Fores, Margarita 241
Fort, Matthew 82, 166
Freddy (son of TPB) 258
free-range meat 9

galangal, *in* Chicken, lime & lemongrass soup 204, *205*
game fowl
    Roast grouse 26, *27*
    Roast woodcock 25
Le Gavroche (restaurant) 48
'Gegs (9-4)' 58
Gentleman's Relish 186
gin, *for* Dry martini 143, *144*
ginger biscuits, *in* Rhubarb fool 138, *139*
ginger (root ginger)
    in Steamed fish, Cantonese-style 247
    in Goan mutton vindaloo 242
    in Sichuan cuisine 229
    in Yellow dhal 246
Glasse, Hannah, *The Art of Cookery Made Plain and Easy* (1747) 136
Goan mutton vindaloo 242
Gong bao chicken 229
Gooseberry fool 138
Goujons of sole, haddock or even pollack 46, *47*
granita, Lemon granita 140
Green's Restaurant and Oyster Bars 43
Grigson, Jane 72
Gruyère cheese
    with French onion soup 60, *61*
    with Pot-au-feu 157
Guacamole 216
guajillo chillies 206

habanero chillies 152, 192, 212, 215, 224, 237
haddock
    in ceviche 220
    Cos & haddock salad *122*, 123
    in Fish pie jr 256
    in goujons 46
haddock (smoked)
    in A really good fish pie 40, *41*
    Haddock Parker Bowles 43
ham, *with* Baked eggs 54
hanging, grouse 26
Haworth, Nigel 82
heart disease, and saturated fats 16
Heath, Ambrose, *Good Savouries* (1934) 133
Hopkinson, Simon 72, 127
Hot toddy 142
Huevos rancheros 57

ice cream
    Affogato 141
    Eccles cake ice cream 82
In-N-Out burger chain 23
Indian dishes
    Goan mutton vindaloo 242
    Rogan josh 244, *245*
    Yellow dhal 246

jaggery (palm sugar) 242
jalapeño peppers 57, 116, 192, 216, 217, 223, 224
James's 'Old Bank' chili 155
Japanese dishes 232-5
John Dory, Asian-style *236*, 237

Karmel, Annabel 249
Kashmiri food, Rogan josh 244, *245*
Keen's Cheddar Ltd 136
kefalotyri cheese 184
kettle barbecue 175, 177
Khanom Jeen Rice Noodles 30
kidneys (lamb's), Devilled, on toast 134
King, Laura 48
King's Ginger liqueur 138
kinilaw 220
Kipper pâté 108
Knott, Bill 48, 179, 244
Kulinarya (2008) 238

Lakeland 162
lamb
  BBQ butterflied leg of lamb 100
  Greek-style roast lamb with macaroni 182, *183*
  Griddled lamb with cucumber raita 98, *99*
  Rack of lamb 97
  Shoulder of lamb with *pommes boulangère* 186
  see also mutton
lamb mince, *in* James's 'Old Bank' chili 155
Laos, street food 203
Larp gai (Laotian chicken salad) 197, 203
Lawson, Nigella 50
Lee, Jeremy 114
leeks, Buttered 118
Leigh, Rowley 48, 68
lemon
  Lemon granita 140
  Lemon risotto 65
lemon juice, for ceviche 223
lemongrass, Chicken, lime & lemongrass soup 204, *205*
lentils
  Lentil salad 261
  Petit salé aux lentilles 179
  see also dhal
lettuce
  Asian steak in lettuce 93
  in Cos & haddock salad *122*, 123
  in Green salad 126
  iceberg, *with* Spicy pork balls 202
  romaine, with *Mole verde* 217
lime juice
  in Chicken, lime & lemongrass soup 204, *205*
  in Green papaya salad 206
Locatelli, Giorgio 64
Loch Duart, salmon 40
Lola (daughter of TPB) 252, 253, 255, 258, 265, 266
Lusty's soups 170

Mabey, Richard, *Food for Free* 137
mackerel, Spiced grilled 106, *107*
The Mail on Sunday (newspaper) 50
Maillard, Louis Camille 150
Manila 238, 241
marinade
  for Asian-style bass, John Dory or other big white fish *236*, 237
  for Boeuf en daube 159
  for Braised venison 171
  for Cochinita pibil 214
  for Gong bao chicken 229
  for Lunch from a late English summer garden 262
marrow bones, *Pot-au-feu* 156
Martin, Mrs, Sticky toffee pudding 72
martini, Dry 143, 144, *145*
May, Robert, *The Accomplisht Cook* 162
Mayonnaise 59
McGee, Harold, *On Food and Cooking* 86, 150
meat, to brown 150
Mexican food 207-227
Mirabeau, Comte de 156
Mole poblano 217
Mole verde 217, *219*
Montgomery's Cheddar 136
mulato chilli 193
mung beans 246
mung beans (split) *see* dhal
mushrooms
  in Big beefy stew 250
  in Boeuf Bourguignon 160
  Chicken & mushroom pie 36, 37
  Mushrooms on toast 137
  Porcini risotto 64
  Porcini with pappardelle 115
  Shiitake *in* Chicken *chanko* 232
mutton
  Goan mutton vindaloo 242
  Rogan josh 244, *245*
  see also lamb

Nahm restaurant (London) 200
Naima (Tunisian cook) 65
Neal Street Restaurant (London) 115
Negroni 146
noodles
  A deeply healthy, utterly addictive noodle dish 30, *31*
  Dan dan noodles *230*, 231
  Lao Söi (curried noodles) 197
  Thai 196
  Udon noodles, *in* Chicken *chanko* 232, *233*
Norwak, Mary, *English Puddings, Sweet and Savoury* 78

Ogden Nash Food (Stewart, Tabori & Chang) 119
onions
  French onion soup 60, *61*
  in Lentil salad 261
  in Tomato salad 63
  in Tortilla 56
  see also red onions; shallots; spring onions
orange juice
  in Bells of St Clements ceviche *222*, 223
  in Big beefy stew 250
  in Cochinita pibil 214
orange (rind of)
  Chocolate & orange soufflés 86, *87*
  Hot cider punch 142

oranges
  Fennel & orange salad 130, *131*
  Orange, red onion & basil salad 132
oregano, in Tom's 10-alarm chili 152
oxtail
  Oxtail consommé (& bullshot) 170
  Oxtail stew 168
  Pot-au-feu 156

pancetta
  Peas with pancetta 94, *95*
  in Penne *all'amatriciana* 180, *181*
  in Ragù alla Bolognese 165
  in Spaghetti alla carbonara 96
  see also bacon
papaya, Green papaya salad 206
paprika
  in Beef Stroganoff 22
  in Rogan josh 244, *245*
Parker Bowles, Brig Andrew (father of TPB) 103, 108
Parker Bowles, Derek H (grandfather of TPB) 43
Parker Bowles, Rosemary 'Rose' (stepmother of TPB) 24, 103, 108, 171
Parmesan cheese
  in Cheesy pasta 259
  with Jeremy's baked asparagus 114
  in Lemon risotto 65
  with Penne *all'amatriciana* 180, *181*
  in Porcini risotto 64
  with Ragù alla Bolognese 165
  with Spaghetti alla carbonara 96
passata, in Mexican beef stew 210
pasta dishes
  Cheesy pasta 259
  Macaroni with Greek-style roast lamb 182, 184, *185*
  Penne all'amatriciana 180, *181*
  Porcini with pappardelle 115
  Ragù alla Bolognese 165
  Red sauce for pasta 263
  Spaghetti bollynaise 251
  Spaghetti alla carbonara 96
  Spaghetti with meatballs 18, *19*
  Tomato & veg pasta sauce 260
pasta stars 251
pastry
  Eccles cakes 80
  feuilles de brick 114
  puff pastry 37
peas
  peas with pancetta 94, *95*
  puréed, *with* Goujons of sole, haddock or even pollack 46
pecorino cheese 184
Penne *all'amatriciana* 180, *181*
Petit salé aux lentilles 179
Philippines
  kinilaw 220
  Sisig (Filipino pork) 238, *239*
Phillips, Roger, *Wild Food* 137
pib (Mexican earth oven) 214
pickles, *with Pot-au-feu* 157
pies
  A really good fish pie 40, *41*

Chicken & mushroom pie 36, 37
Chilli cottage pie 20
pig's head, in Sisig (Filipino pork) 238
pig's trotter, in Boeuf Bourguignon 161
plaice, goujons 46
plums, in Autumn pudding 84, 85
pollack
 in ceviche 220
 in A really good fish pie 256, 257
 in goujons, 46
Polynesia, fish dishes 220
pomegranate, in Bells of St Clements ceviche 222, 223
pork
 alternative for Goan mutton vindaloo 242
 Pulled pork, barbecued 176, 177
pork belly
 Petit salé aux lentilles 179
 Sisig (Filipino pork) 238, 239
pork (minced)
 meatballs 18
 in Ragù alla Bolognese 165
 Sambutes 212, 213
 Spicy pork balls 202
pork ribs, Proper 172, 173
pork rinds, in Boeuf en daube 159
pork shoulder, Cochinita pibil 214
potatoes
 in Fishcakes – good for all ages 258
 with Lola's favourite liver 255
 pommes boulangère, with Shoulder of lamb 186
 Roast potatoes 68
 in Tortilla 56
 in Triple-cooked chips 66
potatoes (baked)
 with caviar 48
 with A simple dish for bachelors and widowers to impress their guests 102, 103
potatoes (mashed)
 in Aligot, 70
 for Chilli cottage pie, 20
 for fish pies, 40, 256
 in Haddock Parker Bowles, 43
Pot-au-feu 156
puddings
 Autumn pudding 84, 85
 Chocolate & orange soufflé 86, 87
 custard 75
 Eccles cake ice cream 82
 Rhubarb fool 138, 139
 Rhubarb & ginger crumble 83
 Sticky toffee pudding 72, 73
 Treacle tart 78, 79
 Trifle 75, 76
Puebla (Mexico) 217
pumpkin seeds, in Mole verde 217

Quintana, Patricia, *The Taste of Mexico* 217
Quo Vadis Restaurant (London) 114

Rabbit & cider casserole *188*, 189
Raspberries, *for* fool 138

red onions
 for ceviches 221, 223, 224
 in Chilli cottage pie 20
 Chilli-pickled red onions 215
 for Guacamole 216
 for Lunch from a late English summer garden 262
 Orange, red onion & basil salad 132
 in Penne all'amatriciana 180, *181*
 in Tom's 10-alarm chili 152, *153*
redcurrants, *in* Autumn pudding 84, 85
rhubarb
 Rhubarb & ginger crumble 83
 Rhubarb fool 138, *139*
rice powder (roasted) 199, 203
rice wine (Shaoxing)
 for Gong bao chicken 229
 with Pot roast chicken 29
risotto
 Lemon risotto 65
 Porcini risotto 64
Roka (Japanese restaurant), 235

Saatchi, Charles 50
salad dressings 119, 120, 123, 124, 126, 130, 132, 199
salads 119-32
 Chicken, liver & chorizo salad 120, *121*
 Cos & haddock salad *122*, 123
 Fennel & orange salad 130, *131*
 Green papaya salad 206
 Green salad 126
 Larp gai (Laotian chicken salad) 197
 Lentil salad 261
 Orange, red onion & basil salad 132
 Oriental cucumber salad *128*, 129
 Provençal green bean salad 127
 Smoked eel & bacon salad 124, *125*
 Thai beef salad *198*, 199
 Tomato salad 63
Salbutes 212
salmon
 Salmon with carrots & tomatoes 257
 in Fish pie jr 256
 in Fishcakes – good for all ages 258
salsas, Mexican 226-7
saltpetre (Prague Powder No 1) 162
Sambutes 212, *213*
sauces
 for barbecued pork 174, 177
 béchamel sauce *for* Fish pie jr 42
 Bread sauce 28
 Chilli fish sauce 32
 for Dan dan noodles 231
 for Gong bao chicken 229
 for Greek-style roast lamb 182, *183*
 for Mole verde 217
 Red sauce for pasta 263
 for Spaghetti with meatballs 18, *19*
 for Spicy pork balls 202
 for Sticky toffee pudding 74
 with Minced beef, chillies & basil 201
 tomato sauce *for* Huevos rancheros 57
 white wine sauce 43
sausages (pork chipolata), *in* Toad in the hole 24

savouries 133-7
Scorsese, Martin, *Goodfellas* 18
Scotch bonnet chillies 20, 129, 212, 215, 223
sea bass
 Asian-style bass, John Dory or other big white fish 236, 237
 Steamed fish, Cantonese-style 247
 in ceviche 220, 223
 Salt-baked sea bass 105
Shand, Philip Morton (great-grandfather to TPB) 20, 133
shellfish
 in A really good fish pie 40
 Avocado prawns, ceviche-style 221
 Clam fritters 109
 Crab cakes 112
 Hot buttered crab 111
 Marinated prawns 110
 Potted shrimps 49
 Shrimp broth 207
 see also ceviches
sherry, with Oxtail consommé (& Bullshot) 170
Sichuan dishes 228-31
 see also China
Sichuan Institute of Higher Cuisine (Chengdu) 228
Sichuan peppers 228, 231
Sisig (Filipino pork) 238, *239*
Slater, Nigel 38
Smith, Delia, 14
Smoked eel & bacon salad, 124, *125*
snapper, *in* Steamed fish, Cantonese-style 247
sole
 in Steamed fish, Cantonese-style 247
 in goujons 46
 Grilled Dover sole 104
soufflés, Chocolate & orange 86, *87*
soups and consommés
 Chicken, lime & lemongrass soup 204, *205*
 Chicken & sweetcorn soup 33
 French onion soup 60, *61*
 Oxtail consommé (& Bullshot) 170
 see also broths
spaghetti
 Spaghetti alla carbonara 96
 Spaghetti Bollynaise 251
 Spaghetti with meatballs 18, *19*
spring onions
 in Steamed fish, Cantonese-style 247
 in Gong bao chicken 229
 in Oriental cucumber salad *128*, 129
 with Yellow dhal 246
 see also onions; shallots
steak 90
 Asian steak in lettuce 93
 fillet steak *in* Beef Stroganoff 22
 Steak (Sirloin) 92
 Thai beef salad *198*, 199
 see also beef; beef (minced)
 stewing steak, *Carbonade flamande* 164
stews
 Big beefy stew 250
 Filipino beef stew (*Adobong baka*) 241

Mexican beef stew 210, *211*
Oxtail stew 168
Sticky toffee pudding 72, *73*
stir-fry
  A deeply healthy, utterly addictive noodle dish 30
  Beef with cumin 200
  Dan dan noodles *230*, 231
stock
  beef stock 160
  chicken stock 38, 71, 186, 189, 204
  Sprouts in stock 71
Stone's Ginger wine 138
street food, Thailand 196-7, 201, 207
Swarbrick, Winnie 80
sweet potatoes
  in Big beefy stew 250
  in Chicken à la Lola 252
  in Veggie mess 264
sweetcorn, *in* Chicken & sweetcorn soup 33

tacos 208
tagliatelle
  Ragù alla Bolognese 165
tamarind water, *in* Green papaya salad 206
Tayag, Claude 241
Temperley, Julian, cider 142
Thai food 196-207
Thompson, David 196, 200
Thurber, James 143
Toad in the hole 24

tofu, *in* Chicken *chanko* 232, *233*
Tolbert, Frank X, *A Bowl of Red* 152
tomatillos (canned), *in* Mole *verde* 217
tomato concassé 43
tomato juice, Bloody Mary 147
tomato
  in Classic ceviche 224
  cherry tomatoes *in* Orange, red onion & basil salad 132
  in Cucumber raita 98
  in Greek-style roast lamb 182, *183*
  in Green papaya salad 206
  in Guacamole 216
  in Huevos rancheros 57
  in Lentil salad 261
  with Penne *all'amatriciana* 180, *181*
  in The perfect burger 23
  in Red sauce for pasta 263
  Salmon with carrots and tomatoes 257
  for salsas 226-7
  in Spaghetti bollynaise 251
  in Spaghetti with meatballs 18
  Tomato & veg pasta sauce 260
  Tomato salad for cauliflower cheese 63
  with Yellow dhal 246
tomme de Cantal, *in* Aligot 70
Tom's 10-alarm chili 152, *153*
Tortilla 56
  with ceviches 224
  Huevos rancheros 57
  with Mexican beef stew 210

in Sambutes 212, *213*
Treacle tart 78, *79*
Trifle 75, 76
Trillin, Calvin 174

veal (minced), *in* Ragù alla Bolognese 165
venison, braised 171
vermouth, for Dry martini 143
vodka, for Vodka martini 143

Wareing, Marcus 89
websites
  www.blackface.co.uk 26
  www.coolchile.co.uk 57, 152, 206, 210, 214, 217
  www.kingsfinefoods.co.uk 48
  www.lakeland.co.uk 162
  www.royalthaisupermarket.com 30
  www.theasiancookshop.co.uk 214
Weir, Caroline and Robin, *Ice Creams, Sorbets & Gelati* 82, 140
whisky, Hot toddy 142
White, Florence, *Good Things in England* (1932) 134
whitecurrants *in* Autumn pudding *84*, 85
Woolf, Virginia, *To the Lighthouse* 159

ya cai, 231
yogurt, *with* Griddled lamb 98, *99*
Yucatán (Mexico) 212, 214

Favourite suppliers

Borough Kitchen www.boroughkitchen.com
A brilliant place for pots, pans, knives, tableware, plus every other kitchen gadget you never knew you needed.

Brown and Forrest www.brownandforrest.co.uk.co.uk
Excellent smoked eel from Somerset, and some pretty fine kippers, trout, bloaters, ham and chicken too.

Cool Chile Co www.coolchile.co.uk
Not just chillies, but all manner of Mexican herbs and spices, plus proper, freshly made corn tortillas.

The Courtyard Dairy www.thecourtyarddairy.co.uk
One of the country's great cheesemongers, The Courtyard Dairy are great champions of British artisan cheese. They're particularly good at promoting local Yorkshire and Lancashire cheesemakers too.

Daylesford www.daylesford.com
Excellent free-range meat, all produced on their own farms, as well as wonderful cheeses, hampers, pies, pottery, broths, stocks and bread.

The Ethical Butcher www.ethicalbutcher.co.uk
High quality, ethically reared meat, all sourced from farms with a regenerative philosophy. Happy beasts mean great flavour, and you'll find all sorts of interesting British producers, as well as some more unusual cuts.

H G Walter www.hgwalter.com
One of the country's finest butchers, all of their meat is free-range, and of the very highest quality. You'll also find offal, stocks, charcuterie, cheese, and all manner of pantry delights.

House of Charcoal www.houseofcharcoal.co.uk
Quite simply the best range of British sustainable charcoal you can find. Lots of different producers, and woods too.

Fortnum and Mason www.fortnumandmason.com
Ok, so I'm a little biased, having written three Fortnum and Mason cookbooks. But this London institution is still at the very top of its game, with everything from tea and coffee to chocolate, hampers, honeys and jams

King's www.kingsfinefoods.co.uk
Caviar. In glorious abundance. Not to mention a whole range of other luxury foods.

Lakeland www.lakeland.co.uk
Cookware, food storage and gadgets galore.

Neals Yard Dairy www.nealsyarddairy.co.uk
The original great British cheesemonger, and still one of the best. Their range of British cheddar is especially excellent.

Sous Chef www.souschef.co.uk
Not just top-quality spices, condiments, vinegar and oils from across the globe, but a good range of cookware, tableware, barbeques and smokers too.

Tireless in the pursuit of a good dinner, award-winning food writer and broadcaster Tom Parker Bowles has concentrated a life spent in thrall to his appetite into one cookbook, *Let's Eat*. The recipes range from the resolutely traditional and British (My mother's roast chicken or the classic Sticky toffee pudding) through the speediest of quick fixes (Steak or Spiced grilled mackerel) to the truly global (Ceviche, Thai beef salad and Mexican beef stew). But all can be easily cooked in the most everyday of kitchens. This is a book about flavour, succour and good cheer. Real food, for people who live to cook and eat.